P9-DID-072

Kids Come in All Languages: Reading Instruction for ESL Students

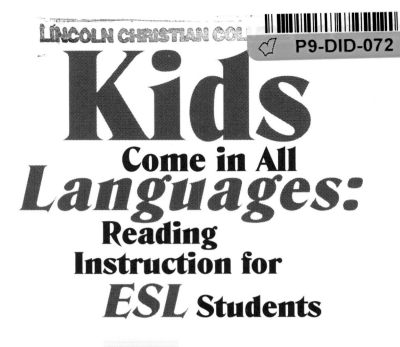

Karen Spangenberg-Urbschat
*Wayne County (MI) Regional
Educational Service Agency*

Robert Pritchard
California State University, Fresno

Editors

International Reading Association
Newark, Delaware 19714, USA

The International Reading Association attempts, through its publications, to provide a forum for a wide spectrum of opinions on reading. This policy permits divergent viewpoints without assuming the endorsement of the Association.

Director of Publications   Joan M. Irwin
Managing Editor   Anne Fullerton
Associate Editor   Chris Celsnak
Assistant Editor   Amy Trefsger
Editorial Assistant   Janet Parrack
Production Department Manager   Iona Sauscermen
Graphic Design Coordinator   Boni Nash
Design Consultant   Larry Husfelt
Desktop Publishing Supervisor   Wendy Mazur
Desktop Publishing   Anette Schuetz-Ruff
                              Cheryl Strum
                              Richard James
Proofing   David Roberts

Library of Congress Cataloging in Publication Data

Spangenberg-Urbschat, Karen.
    Kids come in all languages: Reading instruction for ESL students/
Karen Spangenberg-Urbschat, Robert Pritchard.
        p.   cm.
    Includes bibliographical references and indexes.
        1. English language—Study and teaching—Foreign speakers.
2. Reading.   I. Pritchard, Robert Henry, 1947–   .   II. Title.
PE1128.A2S63   1994   93-48832
428'.007—dc20   CIP
ISBN 0-87207-395-5

Tenth Printing, June 2003

Contents

106334

Foreword

This volume begins to address the pressing need facing the majority of teachers in the United States and in other countries in the English-speaking world—how to teach children whose primary language is not English. Teachers—faced with exploding demographics, lack of knowledge about children's cultures and how languages (first or second or third, oral or written) are learned across different social contexts, lack of pedagogy to restructure the teaching of English language arts for children new to English, and fear of change—need concrete ways of teaching. They also need to learn more about the social and political nature of language use, language learning, and language instruction.

The authors and editors of *Kids Come in All Languages* have long-established commitments to working with teachers and making concrete changes. Change is not easy; nor is it welcomed. But change is inevitable, especially when it is required for addressing the academic needs of children whose primary language is not English. Changing and transforming beliefs, assumptions, and instructional practices related to the teaching and learning process is a formidable task. Confronting and exploring our frustrations, curiosities, and need to know can lead to creating new understandings about the teacher's role in the learning and teaching process, particularly in the "acquisition" of English as a second language.

Organizations such as the International Reading Association need to continue to lead the field in providing forums that address issues of teaching linguistically and culturally diverse children throughout the world. During the past three decades, we have seen a worldwide explosion related to language learning and teaching across contexts, functions, sociopolitical arenas, and the sexes. There are bodies of knowledge in critical pedagogy, whole language, and bilingual education that need to be tapped and shared.

The new pedagogy that is advocated in this much-needed volume is a beginning. *Kids Come in All Languages* attempts to cover the most salient aspects of "English language instruction." But more than just language learning is at stake. Bess Altwerger and Bonnie Ivener highlight the importance of teachers' roles in respecting diversity and knowing how children learn, so that teaching can be organized to facilitate, guide, and mediate learning. If we, the teachers, do not take responsibility for teaching, who will? If we, the teachers, do not learn about how children learn, who will? If we, the teachers, do not change, children will continue to suffer.

The challenges we all face are to learn about learning and teaching, the politics of pedagogy, and the politics of change, and to question our unexamined habitual attitudes that are false and damaging to children, discard them, and transform schooling. It is not just about teaching kids whose primary language is not English. It is not just about learning new techniques or comparing different methods of teaching English as a second language. It is not just about "these problematic immigrant kids." It *is* about paradigmatic change. It is about putting new value on teaching and learning. It is about respecting diversity. It is about shifting the sociopolitical nature of teaching and learning. It is about investing in our children, all our children. It is about practicing democratic beliefs in our pedagogical practices. It is about truly caring.

Language learning and teaching is also about status, power, and voice. Children may ask, "Does my language count? Can I experiment with my language? Is it okay to talk, to ask questions, to voice my opinion? Or are children supposed to be seen and not heard?" Shor (1992) makes us reflect critically on such questions in this passage:

> People begin life as motivated learners, not as passive beings. Children naturally join the world around them. They learn by interacting, by experimenting, and by

using play to internalize the meaning of words and experience. Language intrigues children; they have needs they want met.... But year by year their dynamic learning erodes in passive classrooms not organized around their cultural backgrounds, conditions, or interests. Their curiosity and social instincts decline... (p. 17).

What type of curriculum erodes our students' desire to learn? What type of teaching impedes our students' learning? How can we move away from passive learning and teaching situations? These are just some of the general questions that we should be posing. What are the power relations between teachers and students? What is the status of children's language relative to that of English? Are the children's voices respected? These are more specific questions that need to be addressed in the search for a just pedagogy.

Kids Come in All Languages fills a void with instructional practices that teachers need. It also addresses issues of cultural diversity, challenges commonly held assumptions, and marks a shift to viewing children whose primary language is not English with more respect and dignity. Supporting teachers' pedagogical change is one of the most formidable tasks facing our profession. We need more books such as this.

Barbara Flores
California State University, San Bernardino

Reference

Shor, I. (1992). *Empowering education: Critical teaching for social change.* Chicago, IL: University of Chicago Press.

Contributors

Virginia Garibaldi Allen
The Ohio State
University at Marion
Marion, Ohio

Bess Altwerger
Towson State University
Towson, Maryland

Anna Uhl Chamot
Georgetown University
Arlington, Virginia

Carlos E. Cortés
University of California,
Riverside
Riverside, California

Jim Cummins
Ontario Institute for
Studies in Education
Toronto, Ontario, Canada

Nancy Farnan
San Diego State
University
San Diego, California

James Flood
San Diego State
University
San Diego, California

Georgia Earnest García
University of Illinois at
Urbana–Champaign
Champaign, Illinois

Bonnie Lee Ivener
Albuquerque Public
Schools
Albuquerque, New Mexico

Diane Lapp
San Diego State
University
San Diego, California

Julia Lara
Council of Chief State
School Officers
Washington, D.C.

J. Michael O'Malley
Prince William County
Public Schools
Manassas, Virginia

Robert Pritchard
California State
University, Fresno
Fresno, California

Alfredo Schifini
California State
University, Los Angeles
Los Angeles, California

**Karen Spangenberg-
Urbschat**
Wayne County Regional
Educational Service
Agency
Wayne, Michigan

Eleanor Wall Thonis
Wheatland School District
Wheatland, California

INTRODUCTION

Meeting the Challenge of Diversity

According to recent demographic data, over 2 million limited-English-proficient (LEP) students attend public and private schools in the United States. This number is expected to reach 3.4 million by the year 2000 (Office of Bilingual Education and Minority Language Affairs, 1991), thus greatly increasing the number of students in need of English as a second language (ESL) instruction in U.S. schools. The situation is similar in Canada and, indeed, in many countries where changing immigration patterns have brought learners of other languages to schools in growing numbers. Consequently, the provision of English language and subject matter instruction to ESL students is one of the most critical challenges confronting teachers and teacher educators today.

While the number of ESL students continues to grow dramatically, only a fraction of all ESL students in the United States are in bilingual or ESL classrooms (Olsen, 1988). Consequently, the majority of ESL students receive most, if not all, of their instruction from regular classroom teachers, many of whom have had no specialized training in this area (Enright & McCloskey, 1985). According to a survey conducted by Waggoner and O'Malley (1985), while 25 percent of all public school teachers reported having ESL students in their classrooms, 70 percent of those teachers said they had had no academic preparation in either bilingual or ESL methodology.

1

Regretfully, no evidence exists to indicate that this situation has changed significantly since this study was conducted.

Further exacerbating the situation is the fact that the functions and nature of literacy in today's society have changed. Literacy is no longer defined simply as the ability to read and write. In addition to being able to communicate effectively in oral and written form, to be considered truly literate one must be able to think critically, reason logically, and use technology (Secretary's Commission on Achieving Necessary Skills, 1991). Schools now face pressures to raise standards and change objectives in ways that address this broader definition of literacy. Unfortunately, there is as yet no conclusive evidence to suggest that these efforts have had any significant impact on the type of instruction ESL students receive or on the levels of literacy they subsequently achieve. In fact, there is reason to believe that unless steps are taken, the reforms that have occurred may serve to widen the already substantial gap between the achievement of native speakers of English and those of students from diverse language groups (Olsen & Dowell, 1989).

Although there is a growing consensus that special steps need to be taken if we as educators are to respond successfully to this challenge, there is a disturbing lack of consensus regarding what those steps should be. Unfortunately, the debate does not focus just on pedagogical issues, but on political, economic, and social considerations as well.

This book grew out of our need to address what we believe is the single most significant educational issue resulting from the changes in school populations and approaches: how to help students from language-minority backgrounds develop literacy in English. The purpose of this book is to identify and answer the major questions surrounding reading instruction for ESL students. Specifically, this book does the following:

- reviews and synthesizes what we know about background issues related to the education of ESL students;

- provides specific suggestions to teachers and administrators for organizing for instruction and enhancing student learning; and
- gives concrete examples of practical ways in which teachers can develop and implement authentic, meaning-centered, instructional activities.

The first three chapters of *Kids Come in All Languages* provide a succinct discussion of some of the issues that now—or soon will—confront teachers, schools, and school boards. The demographic data presented in chapter 1 indicate that the numbers of culturally and linguistically diverse students in the U.S. are rapidly rising. Author Julia Lara identifies the challenges that result from these demographic trends as well as the ramifications of failing to address them. In chapter 2, Carlos Cortés stresses acceptance of students' home language, culture, and ethnicity, and presents his "multiculturation model" that incorporates these concepts. His explanation of the model and its relationship to reading and language arts instruction will enable students and teachers to gain insight into their right to and need for empowerment. The third chapter discusses the issue of what constitutes sufficient time for English language acquisition. Author Jim Cummins maintains that more than a superficial understanding of vocabulary and sentence structure is required if students are to comprehend the academic content areas of the curriculum.

Our goal in section 2 is to consider three of the most important factors that teachers must address as they organize for instruction. In chapter 4, Bess Altwerger and Bonnie Lee Ivener explain the relationship between self-esteem and the achievement of ESL students. The authors stress the importance of accepting and respecting diversity in the classroom and explain the ways a whole language perspective can facilitate learning. The fifth chapter presents an overview of teaching procedures and instructional approaches that research has shown to be effective in meeting the needs of ESL students. Anna Chamot and Michael O'Malley provide practical ideas for implementing these suggestions in instructional settings. The importance of using authentic materials from a variety of genres is the focus of chapter 6. In addition, author Virginia Allen offers selection criteria and an extensive bibliography specifically designed for teachers of ESL students.

The chapters in section 3 focus on instructional practices. In the seventh chapter, Nancy Farnan, James Flood, and Diane Lapp discuss the integration of reading and writing and its implications for ESL instruction. They then present instructional activities and materials that are consistent with this integrated perspective. Chapter 8 contains concrete suggestions for reducing the complexity of expository text for ESL students. Alfredo Schifini's treatment of expository text structure as well as vocabulary and concept development will generate deeper understandings of the ways in which teachers can facilitate their ESL students' comprehension of expository text. Assessment of language-minority students has long been a difficult task due to a dearth of appropriate tests, qualified examiners, and guidelines for program inclusion and exclusion. Complications such as these are discussed by Georgia García in the ninth chapter of this book. She offers suggestions for more authentic means of assessing student performance on an ongoing basis.

The book concludes with a short discussion by Eleanor Thonis of some contemporary research on language and literacy development. She leaves the reader with thought-provoking questions and the realization that many issues remain unresolved.

In *Kids Come in All Languages,* we have attempted to provide a balanced view of reading instruction for ESL students. Obviously, much more could be said about this topic. We realize that many issues remain to be researched, written about, debated, researched and debated again, and finally resolved in practice—only to be researched again. We encourage others to continue to investigate this area and work to develop effective instructional and assessment practices for ESL students. As the numbers and diversity of these students increase, educators everywhere will need to seek solutions, meet challenges, and embrace changes necessary to ensure quality education for all students. Our hope is that this book will contribute to that effort.

RP

KSU

References

Enright, D.S., & McCloskey, M.L. (1985). Yes, talking! Organizing the classroom to promote second language acquisition. *TESOL Quarterly, 15,* 431–453.

Office of Bilingual Education and Minority Language Affairs. (1991). *SEA Title VII data report summary counts: School year 1989–1990*. Washington, DC: U.S. Department of Education.

Olsen, L. (1988). *Immigrant students and the California public schools: Crossing the schoolhouse border.* San Francisco, CA: California Tomorrow.

Olsen, L., & Dowell, C. (1989). *Bridges: Promising programs for the education of immigrant children.* San Francisco, CA: California Tomorrow.

Secretary's Commission on Achieving Necessary Skills. (1991). *What work requires of schools: A SCANS report for America 2000.* Washington, DC: U.S. Department of Labor.

Waggoner, D., & O'Malley, J.M. (1985). Teachers of limited-English-proficient children in the United States. *NABE: The Journal of the National Association for Bilingual Education, 9*(3), 25–42.

Section 1

Issues

We begin this book with a consideration of some of the major issues that affect the teaching of English to speakers of other languages (referred to in this book as "ESL" students). Among these is the rapidly changing demography of the United States and its schools. Chapter 1 discusses the dimensions and implications of these changes in school population as well as possible federal, state, and local responses to them. Although the focus here is on the United States, the American experience does have parallels in other English-speaking countries where changing patterns of immigration are bringing more ESL learners into school systems.

Chapter 2 addresses the issue of how our classrooms can benefit from the cultural and linguistic diversity ESL students bring. The effects of this diversity, which permeates and influences the instructional setting, are multifaceted and far reaching. The challenge that teachers face is to ensure that these effects are positive. Although the focus in this chapter is again on the United States, the information presented has relevance for all those working with learners from diverse backgrounds.

Both first- and second-language acquisition can and should involve active, constructive processes in which learners are driven by the need and desire to communicate. However, unlike the development of native-language proficiency, second-language acquisition frequently occurs in unnatural contexts that emphasize linguistic accuracy rather than communicative fluency. Chapter 3 presents suggestions that will enable teachers to establish and maintain learning settings that reverse this pattern.

Julia Lara

Demographic Overview: Changes in Student Enrollment in American Schools

Educators in the United States are becoming increasingly aware of the changes in the racial and ethnic composition of the nation's public school population. Since the late 1970s public schools have experienced a dramatic growth in the enrollment of ethnic- and language-minority students. Although total school enrollment declined by 2 percent between 1976 and 1988, the proportion of minorities increased by 23 percent in that period. In 1990 African Americans, Latinos, Amerindians, and Asians made up 32 percent of the total public school enrollment in the nation, and 33 of the largest school districts had an enrollment of over 50 percent ethnic- and language-minority students (National Center for Education Statistics, 1993). By the end of the century minority students will make up almost 42 percent of total public school enrollment (Commission on Minority Participation in Education and American Life, 1988).

Particularly striking has been the rate of growth for Hispanic and Asian students. As shown in Table 1, these groups represent the segment of the school-age population showing the greatest growth in enrollment. Between 1980 and 1991 enrollment of Hispanic students increased by 48 percent, making it 12 percent of total enrollment for kindergarten to grade 12; during the same period, enrollment of Asians and Pacific Islanders increased by 84 percent, making it 3 percent of the total K to 12 enrollment (National Center for Education Statistics, 1993). Although Hispanics, Asians, and Pacific Islanders form the largest segments of the non-native-English–speaking population in the nation and in the schools, the number of native speakers of Arabic, Armenian, Polish, Haitian Creole, and Russian also increased during the 1980s (McArthur, 1991). The result is a greater variety of languages and cultures in U.S. classrooms.

Language-minority students come from homes where languages other than English are the primary ones spoken. The English-language skills of language-minority students range from none to fluency. For educators, the increase in the cultural and linguistic diversity of the school-age population presents a significant challenge. Considering the pattern of low academic achievement among minority students generally and among subgroups of the language-minority population in particular, there is cause for concern. The following indicators from the National Assessment of Educational Progress (1990) demonstrate the severity of the minority-student underachievement problem:

> The average reading, math and science achievement of black and Hispanic students from the elementary through high school years is below the performance of white students. Results from the National Assessment of Educational Progress (NAEP, 1990) show that the gap in performance between black and white high school students (17 years old) in reading was 20 points; in math 29 points; and science 45 points. Similarly, the gap in performance between Hispanics and white high school students was 24 points in reading; 24 points in mathematics; and 38 points in science.

Table 1
Enrollment in U.S. Public Schools by Race/Ethnicity

Race/Ethnicity	Number in Thousands		Percent Change, 1980–1991
	1980	1991	
Total	39,832	40,847	+ 2
White, non-Hispanic	29,180	27,727	– 5
Total minority	10,651	13,119	+ 23
Black, non-Hispanic	6,418	6,616	+ 3
Hispanic	3,179	4,715	+ 48
Asian/Pacific Islander	749	1,379	+ 84
American Indian/Alaskan Native	305	409	+ 34

Race/Ethnicity	Percent of Public School Enrollment	
	1980	1991
White, non-Hispanic	73	68
Total minority	27	32
Black, non-Hispanic	16	16
Hispanic	8	12
Asian/Pacific Islander	2	3
American Indian/Alaskan Native	1	1

Data from U.S. Department of Education (1980, 1993). Note: Columns may not add up to total because of rounding.

Focusing exclusively on the language characteristics of the minority-student population, the National Coalition of Advocates for Students (1988) says that "Immigrant students, most of whom are language minorities, are more likely than nonimmigrant students to be retained in grade and placed in low academic tracks on the basis of language barrier or low academic progress."

The challenge posed by ethnic and linguistic diversity is heightened when the underachievement problem is considered in relation to workforce needs of a changing economy. The National Alliance of Business (1992) reported that more than half of small business owners have trouble finding entry level workers with even the basic skills in reading, writing, and computation. The fastest growing occupations require workers with higher levels of mathematics, language, and reasoning capabilities (Secretary's Commission on Achieving Necessary Skills, 1991). Manufacturing jobs, a source of employment for significant numbers of minority adults, are declining. Therefore, there will be few employment opportunities for low-skilled individuals to enter the job market. Given that a greater proportion of the U.S. workforce of the future will be nonwhite and immigrant, it is clear that a significant number of potentially at-risk minority students will need to achieve higher levels of literacy to meet the workforce demands of the future.

Contributing Factors

Two important demographic trends have contributed to these dramatic changes in public school enrollment: immigration and fertility rates. Prior to the 1960s, immigration policies in place in the United States gave preference to individuals from western Europe. However, 1965 amendments to immigration legislation eliminated quotas and reduced emphasis on accepting immigrants with high levels of skill and education. These changes, an increase in the number of refugee visas issued, and political turmoil in Central America and Southeast Asia resulted in the current wave of immigration to the United States. In the 1980s the primary sources of immigrants to the United States were Asia (42 percent) and Latin America (42 percent); Europeans dropped to 11 percent of all immigrants (O'Hare & Felt, 1991). In addition, birthrates among minority women in general and Hispanic women in particular have contributed to changes in school enrollment. In 1990, the fertility rate for Hispanic women was 108 per thousand; for black women it was 85; for white women it was 67; and for Asian and Pacific Islander women it was 68 (National Center for Health Statistics, 1991). Not only are some minority women having more children than white women, they have their first children earlier and therefore will probably have babies for a longer period of time.

Language Issues

How well students adjust to their school environment and whether they ultimately succeed academically depends on their individual characteristics and the support provided by their families, the school system, and society in general. In considering what types of instructional and non-instructional services need to be provided to language-minority students, it is necessary to understand the problems that face them and affect their educational well-being. These may include low income and low educational attainment in addition to language factors.

For educators, one of the most important indicators of a probable need for English-language support among language-minority children is a high frequency of native-language use in the home. An analysis of the 1990 census reports reveals that 45 percent of the Spanish-speaking respondents over five years of age used Spanish "all the time" or "more often" than English. For Asians, the frequency of native-language use in the home was high for 47 percent of the respondents (McArthur, 1991). Another indicator is the number of school age children (5- to 17-year-olds) who reported not speaking English well or at all in the 1990 census survey: 16 percent of all Spanish speakers and 16 percent of all Asian language speakers (U.S. Census

Bureau, 1990). Thus, it appears that within the overall population the frequency of native-language use is high. This has implications for the design of English-language instructional services and of approaches that incorporate the students' native language.

Not all language-minority students have limited literacy skills in English, but for many students, lack of English-language skills places them at risk of school failure. This is particularly the case when schools are unable to provide appropriate language-learning experiences.

Students in need of language-support services are generally identified at the local level through a series of assessment procedures designed to determine the level of English ability (understand, speak, read, or write) of language minority students. The identification criteria define what constitutes limited English proficiency and are used to determine whether a student is eligible for program services (bilingual education, ESL, content ESL, and so on). Students who do not meet the established proficiency criteria are classified as limited English proficient (LEP); those who are not so classified are placed in English-only classrooms. All students classified as LEP should be provided with language-support services. However, in some states there is a discrepancy between the number of LEP students identified and the number served. This means that some students may not be receiving any language-support services.

According to figures collected at the local level and reported to state education agencies, the total number of LEP students served in the United States is more than 2.4 million (see Table 2). However, observers believe that this figure underestimates the actual number of LEP students enrolled in the public schools and suggest the number is between 2 million and 3.5 million students, depending on the definition of "limited English proficient." The actual number of LEP students in the United States is not known because the standards for identification vary among, and within, the states. While all states have established procedures to identify these students, local districts have flexibility in selecting the assessment procedures to be used, types of tests, and cut-off points on these tests. As a consequence, a student who is identified as LEP in one state might not qualify in another state. Moreover, districts may report to the state education agencies the number of students served rather than the number of students *in need* of services.

In spite of these serious limitations, federal and state agencies use counts of LEP students as indicators of the numbers of limited-English-proficient students in the United States. These numbers are reported to the federal government and are used for a variety of purposes, including decisionmaking about disbursement of federal dollars to states and local districts. At the state level these figures are also used to determine funding and to develop programs to meet the needs of this population.

Table 2 shows LEP counts based on numbers collected by the state departments of education. Nationally, LEP-student enrollment has increased by 56 percent between 1985 and 1992 (U.S. Department of Education, 1993). Spanish speakers are in the majority (75 percent), followed by speakers of Asian languages (12 percent) and other languages. The "other" category includes Native Americans and speakers of European languages and Arabic. Although the language-minority student population is concentrated in a few states, all but five states have experienced some growth in the number of LEP students enrolled in their schools. Moreover, in 25 states LEP-student enrollments have increased by 50 percent or more over this four-year period.

The impact of ethnic- and language-minority student enrollment varies among regions. Most of the enrollment increases have occurred in Texas, California, Florida, North Carolina, and Arizona. All of these states have high minority birthrates and, except for North Carolina, high immigration rates. Although Illinois and New York are located in regions where overall enrollment has been declining, enrollment of Hispanic and Asian students is expected to increase as a result of immigration. Therefore, the proportion of students from Hispanic and Asian backgrounds in the total school population will also increase. Minority student enrollment exceeds white enrollment in Texas and California. In another 13 states minority students comprise at least one-third of all youths under 18 (Center for the Study of Social Policy, 1993).

Impact on the Schools

Increased enrollment of immigrant and native-born language-minority students presents new challenges to school systems across the United States. These include overcrowding, lack of funds, and disruption as all members of the school community adjust to the change. However, the greatest difficulty facing the schools as they respond to changing enrollment is the shortage of qualified bilingual and ESL teachers. Moreover, teachers who understand languages other than Spanish are rare. Although Spanish is the language of the greatest proportion of LEP students, more than one foreign language is spoken in 64 percent of schools with LEP students (U.S. Department of Education, 1991). In California, 22,365 bilingual and ESL teachers will be needed to prepare the state's 860,000 language-minority students to participate effectively in the mainstream English-language economy (California Department of Education, 1991). Many school districts have initiated aggressive recruitment of bilingual teachers to accommodate the rising enrollment of immigrant LEP students. One example is the Los Angeles school district, where bilingual teachers are paid as much as $5,000 a year more than the regular starting salary ("A special report," 1991).

As a result of the teacher shortage, many schools are providing ESL instruction without support in students' native languages. Students whose country of origin is Laos, Cambodia, or Thailand are particularly at risk because there are very few teachers who speak Lao, Hmong, or Khmer. Students may receive an hour or two of ESL instruction per day but are often mainstreamed into an all-English classroom for mathematics, science, and social studies instruc-

Table 2
LEP Student Enrollment Reported in U.S. Public Schools

	1985–1986	1991–1992	6-year increase
LEP students	1,491,304	2,326,548	56%
Total K-12 students	39,422,050	38,074,628	-3%
Percentage LEP	4%	6%	
By State or District			
Alabama	70	1,671	228%
Alaska	10,471	12,058	15%
Arizona	38,747	67,395	74%
Arkansas	360		
California	567,564	1,073,705	89%
Colorado	16,025	25,028	56%
Connecticut	10,660	16,703	57%
Delaware	1,184	1,929	63%
District of Columbia	4,409	3,461	-22%
Florida	34,326	97,288	183%
Georgia	3,910	7,056	80%
Hawaii	8,836	10,433	18%
Idaho	1,990	4,980	150%
Illinois	58,327	87,178	49%
Indiana	2,839	4,822	70%
Iowa	3,228	4,265	32%
Kansas	6,485	6,066	-6%
Kentucky	1,071	1,544	44%
Louisiana	8,877	8,339	-6%
Maine	900	1,562	74%
Maryland	7,020	12,101	72%
Massachusetts	25,660	42,693	66%
Michigan	14,008	36,720	162%
Minnesota	9,461	18,769	98%
Mississippi	1,291	1,748	35%
Missouri	3,156	3,838	22%
Montana	2,738	6,374	133%
Nebraska	917	1,806	97%
Nevada	3,401	10,804	214%
New Hampshire	342	1,064	211%
New Jersey	37,650	45,204	20%
New Mexico	50,772	64,307	27%
New York	140,545	106,484	-24%
North Carolina	3,000	7,026	134%
North Dakota	6,448	8,076	25%
Ohio	9,760	10,596	9%
Oklahoma	6,993	16,393	134%
Oregon	3,968	12,005	203%
Pennsylvania	12,193		

continued on next page

Table 2
LEP Student Enrollment Reported in U.S. Public Schools
(*continued*)

	1985–1986	1991–1992	6-year increase
Rhode Island	5,227	7,549	44%
South Carolina	203	1,395	587%
South Dakota	5,489	5,848	7%
Tennessee	2,100	2,509	19%
Texas	274,091	331,054	21%
Utah	9,408	23,508	150%
Vermont	512	550	7%
Virginia	9,000		
Washington	17,151	33,904	98%
West Virginia	300e		
Wisconsin	8,354	14,576	74%
Wyoming	1,835	1,705	-7%

Notes:
blank = LEP student enrollment not reported
e = estimated
Source: U.S. Department of Education, OBEMLA

tion. Olsen and Chen (1988) estimate that in California 9 percent of all immigrant language-minority students do not receive ESL support at all. As one student reported, "I just sat in my classes and didn't understand anything."

The shortage of specially trained teachers is a critical problem facing schools with high numbers of LEP children, but public schools are also in need of school counselors, psychologists, nurses, paraprofessionals, and front office personnel who can communicate with students in their native language, or who are trained to work sensitively with ethnically and linguistically diverse populations. There is also a need to increase the number of minority teachers. While classrooms are becoming ethnically diverse, the U.S. teaching force is increasingly white. In 1990, 86 percent of all teacher-education students were white, and this trend is expected to continue despite attempts to recruit more minorities into the profession (Council of Great City Schools, 1993).

Federal and State Support

Although many U.S. school districts may experience difficulty in responding effectively to these demographic changes, some assistance is available from state and federal governments. At the federal level, programs such as Bilingual Education (Title VII), the Emergency Immigrant Education Program, and the Transitional Program for Refugee Children are sources of funds to serve LEP students. Other federal sources of funds include Chapter 1, special education, and migrant and vocational education programs. State funding for bilingual and ESL programs exceeds federal support in some states. For example, in Texas only 10 percent of all services to LEP students is funded by the federal bilingual-education program; in New York, the amount is 23 percent, and in New Jersey it is 3 percent (Council of Chief State School Officers, 1991).

Meeting the Challenge

In order to meet the challenge that linguistically diverse students present to schools, changes will be required at all levels of government as well as within school systems. Federal and state governments will need to expand the level of financial support provided to schools. They will also need to provide policy guidance to school districts and expand their data collection and analysis efforts so that educators will be better prepared to develop programs for these students. At the local level, school systems must fulfill their responsibilities of identifying language-minority students; assessing their proficiency in both English and their native language; placing them in language-support programs; providing content area instruction through native-language or content-based ESL approaches; and systematically evaluating the English-language development and academic performance of these students.

At the classroom level, modifications are needed in what is taught, the manner in which teachers organize and deliver instruction to students, and the way teachers assess student learning. Moreover, there is ample evidence of the need to make instruction more culturally sensitive. Finally, without the support of the home, efforts undertaken by school personnel will be less successful and will perhaps fail. Schools and parents need to form partnerships and build stronger links between home and school. Communities in many areas have begun to establish these links. However, given the demographic forces shaping the schools, much more needs to be done.

References

A special report: Numbers please. (1991, April 8). *New York Times*.

California Department of Education. (1991). *Remedying the shortage of teachers for limited English proficient students*. Sacramento, CA: author.

Center for the Study of Social Policy. (1993). *Kids count data book*. Washington, DC: author.

Commission on Minority Participation in Education and American Life. (1988). *One-third of a nation*. Washington, DC: American Council on Education and Education Commission of the States.

Council of Chief State School Officers. (1991). *School success for limited English proficient students*. Washington, DC: author.

Council of Great City Schools. (1993). Diversifying our great city school teachers: Twenty year trend. *Urban Indicator, 1*(2), 1-7.

McArthur, E. (1991). *Language and schooling in the U.S.: A changing picture 1979–1980*. Washington, DC: National Center for Education Statistics.

National Alliance of Business. (1992). *Real jobs for real people: An employers guide to youth apprenticeship*. Washington, DC: author.

National Assessment of Educational Progress. (1990). *Accelerating academic achievement: A summary of findings from 20 years of NAEP*. Washington, DC: U.S. Department of Education, Office of Educational Research and Improvement.

National Center for Education Statistics. (1993). *The condition of education*. Washington, DC: U.S. Department of Education, Office of Educational Research and Improvement.

National Center for Health Statistics. (1991). *Advance report of final national statistics*. Washington, DC: author.

National Coalition of Advocates for Students. (1988). *New voices: Immigrant students in U.S. public schools*. Boston, MA: author.

O'Hare, W.P., & Felt, J.C. (1991). Asian Americans: America's fastest growing minority group. In *Population trends and public policy*. Washington, DC: Population Reference Bureau.

Olsen, L., & Chen, M.T. (1988). *Crossing the schoolhouse border: Immigrant students and the California public schools*. San Francisco, CA: California Tomorrow.

Secretary's Commission on Achieving Necessary Skills. (1991). *What work requires of schools: A SCANS report for America 2000*. Washington, DC: U.S. Department of Labor.

U.S. Census Bureau. (1990). Fertility of American women: June 1990. *Current Population Reports* (Series P-20, no. 454). Washington, DC: author.

U.S. Department of Education. (1980). *Data from a state summary of elementary and secondary school civil rights survey—1980*. Washington, DC: U.S. Office for Civil Rights.

U.S. Department of Education. (1991). *The condition of bilingual education in the nation*. Washington, DC: author.

U.S. Department of Education. (1993, February). *Adjusted national estimated data from an elementary and secondary school civil rights survey—1990*. Washington, DC: U.S. Office for Civil Rights.

Carlos E. Cortés

2

Multiculturation: An Educational Model for a Culturally and Linguistically Diverse Society

The United States has reached a critical moment in its history. The nation's growing racial, ethnic, cultural, and linguistic diversity, spurred greatly by immigration (particularly from Asia and Latin America), has brought new opportunities and challenges. Moreover, it has given renewed significance to the national motto, *e pluribus unum*—out of many, one, or more broadly, out of diversity, unity. So what does that motto mean for the future of the increasingly multiethnic United States?

Let us begin by examining what the motto does not mean. It does not just say *"pluribus"*—everybody go off and do your own thing, separate yourselves from other Americans, live in your own racial, ethnic, cultural, religious, or neighborhood cocoons, create barriers to exclude those different from you, disregard the needs and rights of others, and ignore those elements that bind the nation together. A total emphasis is on diversity without consideration of the need to foster unity provides a formula for anarchy and societal fragmentation. But the motto also does not just say "*unum*"—everybody should be alike, think alike, believe alike, and act alike. And it certainly does not suggest that everybody will learn alike. It does not call on members of American society to become monocultural clones, nor does it justify punishing people because of their differences or attempting to suppress ethnic and cultural practices or languages. Moreover, pure *unum* is as impossible as pure *pluribus* is untenable, because history has forged the United States into a land of diverse races, diverse religions, diverse ethnicities, and diverse cultures.

The very origin of the United States mitigated against pure *unum*, because Europeans came to a land where hundreds of American Indian civilizations already flourished. The English colonies continued to erode the possibility of pure *unum* when they imported black slaves from Africa, and the independent United States expanded pluralism when it grabbed one-half of Mexico's land, simultaneously annexing 80,000 Mexicans and tens of thousands of Indians. Pure *unum* receded even further as millions of immigrants poured into the United States from southern and eastern Europe, Latin America, and Asia.

While pure *pluribus* without *unum* would be a formula for anarchy, any concerted effort to impose pure *unum*—given the pluralistic heritage, current multicultural reality, and the inevitable increase in the ethnic diversity of the U.S.—would require radical cultural (as well as political, social, and economic) oppression. But even then it would probably fail, in light of the worldwide evidence of the depth of cultural tenacity, ethnic loyalties, linguistic pride, and religious convictions that often survive in the face of extreme efforts by some governments to penalize, suppress, or eradicate such differences. Moreover, the racial diversity of the United States makes a mockery of the proverbial melting pot, in which people of color were never meant to be included. Powerful American pluralism, which is constantly renewed by racially, culturally, and linguistically diverse immigration, simply will not succumb to unity-oriented extremism.

But with pure *pluribus* and pure *unum* equally illusory, unworkable, and undesirable, society faces the challenge of seeking a positive, constructive, and dynamic balance of these two poles. Schools play a critical role in meeting that challenge, as they must prepare students—including students from culturally and linguistically diverse backgrounds—to become effective and sensitive contributors to society. Reading and other language arts teachers have a vital role to play in helping to shape a viable, equitable, 21st-century version of *e pluribus unum.*

But how? How can teachers engage pluralistic social realities—racial differences, the constancy of immigration, the tenacity of cultures, the diversity of values, and the multiplicity of languages spoken—while at the same time trying to help forge a unity that binds people together? Nations around the world are simultaneously grappling with this issue, and the explosions of ethnic violence, racial tension, cultural conflict, and religious intolerance suggest the dimensions of the challenge.

For the past two decades I have been pondering the unavoidable pluralism/unity dilemmas of a multicultural United States, with a special focus on the role that schools can and should play. To address this issue, I have developed an educational model-in-progress for a diverse society. I call it *multiculturation,* a convenient blending of *multiple* and *acculturation.* The multiculturation model combines three essential characteristics:

1. Dynamism—the need and willingness to continuously adapt this model to meet changing societal conditions and to incorporate new educational ideas and research.

2. Empowerment—the dual goals of helping all persons living in the United States to develop the qualities essential for living up to their human potential while simultaneously helping to

strengthen American institutions, communities (both geographical and cultural), states, and the nation.

3. Mutual accommodation—the challenge of and commitment to helping *all* persons and institutions in the United States to acculturate successfully to their rapidly changing nation and the shrinking globe.

Multiculturation, in short, calls for the continuous mutual acculturation of people, cultures, and institutions in the United States, based on the quest for positive basic commonalities, the recognition and nourishment of constructive differences, and the building of a better nation based on the strengths of both unity and diversity.

My multiculturation educational model has four elements, each of which has applications to language arts instruction in general and reading instruction in particular:

1. Mainstream empowerment acculturation—the development of the capacities of all students to function more effectively as part of the mainstream.

2. Intergroup understanding acculturation—the development of the capacities of all students to function with intercultural knowledge, understanding, and sensitivity in an increasingly racially, ethnically, culturally, and linguistically diverse society.

3. Group resource acculturation—the development of individual and societal resources by drawing on—not attempting to eradicate—student ethnic, cultural, and linguistic resources.

4. Civic commitment acculturation—the development of students' sense of concern for and commitment to others and willingness to act on the basis of that caring in order to work toward a more just, equitable society.

Let us explore each of these four types of acculturation. In the process, I will suggest the special and critical role that reading and other aspects of language arts education can play in their acquisition.

Mainstream Empowerment Acculturation

Notice I use the word acculturation, not assimilation. As I employ the two terms, acculturation means learning to *adapt* to mainstream culture, while assimilation means attempting to *adopt* it as yours. While assimilation is subtractive—as when schools encourage students to leave their ethnic and cultural differences behind and sometimes even to hide or escape from those differences—acculturation is additive because it involves encouraging students to learn to operate within the mainstream while at the same time participating, if they wish, in their various cultures. Assimilation at the societal level involves the untenable eradication of cultural differences, the wasteful suppression of linguistic differences, and the impossible goal of eliminating racial identities. Such melting-pot assimilation has never worked for all Americans, particularly nonwhite Americans. Moreover, its chances of working grow weaker as the nation becomes increasingly multiethnic.

Mainstream empowerment acculturation, then, does not demand the assimilative destruction or rejection of cultural differences. Rather it involves helping students to develop new capabilities. It means helping students to acquire socially unifying beliefs, values, and loyalties. It involves helping students to develop effective oral and written English and critical thinking ability. (In the words of Edmund Burke, "To read without reflecting is like eating without digesting.") It encompasses helping students to acquire enriching knowledge, societal understanding, and the multiple skills that will enable them to have a reasonable chance of taking advantage of opportunities and attaining the fabled American dream. It involves educating all people of the United States, including those who come from non-English-speaking backgrounds, about mainstream

American culture and helping them to develop an understanding of when, where, how, and why they need to follow mainstream norms rather than drawing on their own ethnic and cultural norms and behaviors in inappropriate situations. (I call this *situational cultural appropriateness*.)

Mainstream empowerment acculturation requires more than merely opening school doors, providing seats in a classroom, and offering basic education. It means more than removing discriminatory barriers to opportunity or exhorting students to succeed. Rather it should focus on fostering real lifelong opportunity.

Take the role of reading instruction and other elements of language arts education. We cannot be satisfied simply with raising high school graduation rates or improving reading-test scores, because diplomas and basic skills alone are little more than a one-way street to a life of limited opportunity in an increasingly high-tech working world. Instead, reading education should involve going the extra mile or miles in helping students to become truly empowered with knowledge, skills (including critical thinking), and language abilities (including forceful oral and written English expression), so that they can take advantage of opportunities and become fully equipped and effective members of society. Equity through mainstream empowerment acculturation, then, forms the first element of educational multiculturation for limited-English speakers as well as for other students.

Intergroup Understanding Acculturation

Intergroup understanding acculturation includes the ability to feel comfortable amidst cultural, racial, ethnic, linguistic, accent, and other kinds of individual and group differences. It includes the skills of understanding and relating to people with different cultural norms, values, and forms of behavior, as well as recognizing and comprehending multiple cultural perspectives on historical themes and contemporary issues. It includes the capacity to address with insight the inevitable intercultural dilemmas inherent in a multiethnic society such as the United States.

Such pluralism acculturation is essential for all members of U.S. society, from descendants of English colonists to new Latin American and Asian immigrants and refugees. Whatever their backgrounds, students of today, adults of the future, need this empowering intercultural knowledge and these skills and attitudes. To be truly ready for the future, all Americans will need both intergroup and mainstream capabilities.

What does this mean for schools? To work toward real student pluralistic empowerment, all schools need to institute a conscious, continuous, and constructive process of K to 12 multicultural education in order to help prepare students to live with multicultural literacy, sensitivity, and abilities. It requires the "multiculturalizing" of college and university curricula, including an increased emphasis on multiculturalism in teacher education. And it requires ongoing remedial multicultural inservice education for current teachers, most of whom have not benefited from K to 12 or university multicultural education.

This multicultural teacher and inservice education should include the improvement of intercultural understanding, the development of strategies for working with culturally and linguistically diverse students, and the multicultural integration of the curriculum. This is no one-shot workshop-type training; all teachers need ongoing strengthening of their multicultural knowledge, skills, and attitudes, because new waves of immigration and demographic changes will continuously alter the nature of U.S. multiethnicity. But as British historian E.L. Woodward pointed out, "Everything good has to be done over again, forever."

Reading instruction should be integral to student empowerment through intergroup understanding acculturation. This necessitates the careful selection of reading materials that expose students to cultural diversity. Remember Plato's warning: "Those who tell the stories also rule the society." Reading instructors need to be trained in techniques to help students derive intercultural insights from these materials and learn to make nuanced, evidence-based generalizations about ethnic and cultural groups without falling into the rigid distortions of stereotyping.

Many educators have argued that, for purposes of strengthening self-identity, students need to encounter reading material that reflects their own cultures and backgrounds. While this is true, it is also vital that they be exposed to materials that provide them with insights into the experiences and cultures of others with whom they will come into contact. Salvadoran immigrants need to learn about Cambodian culture and the Cambodian American experience. Russian immigrants need to learn about Haitian culture and the Haitian American experience. Reading education provides an ideal avenue for such learning. Whereas reading instruction can serve the function of promoting mainstream empowerment by helping students to develop critical thinking skills and a better understanding of American core values, it can also promote pluralistic acculturation by helping students to develop a better understanding of the diverse groups and cultures that increasingly make up American society.

But a word of warning is in order here. Reading teachers should make certain that their selections and assignments present the perspectives of ethnic insiders, not only observing outsiders; that is, they should be sure that assigned reading includes books *by* members of different ethnic, cultural, and racial groups, not just books *about* those groups. In the myriad lists of children's books about culture and ethnicity that I have encountered, I have often been disappointed—even shocked—by the overwhelming and sometimes exclusive presence of books and stories that present outsiders' visions with little or no appearance of insiders' views. To achieve balance and validity in intergroup understanding acculturation, teachers need to have students read insiders' reactions as well as outsiders' observations.

Diversity need not lead to divisiveness, but the failure to promote intercultural understanding virtually guarantees it. The United States cannot afford a society like that described by Rudyard Kipling when he wrote, "All the people like us are We, and everyone else is They." Reading instruction can make a significant contribution to a better pluralistic society through intergroup understanding acculturation.

Group Resource Acculturation

Robert Maynard Hutchins, former president of the University of Chicago, once said, "The best education for the best is the best education for all"—a vision I support. However, we must also heed the perceptive words of the former U.S. Supreme Court Chief Justice Oliver Wendell Holmes when he perceptively warned, "There is nothing as unequal as the equal treatment of unequals." Therein lies the challenge—to provide the best education for all, while at the same time recognizing the existence of individual and group differences that influence the process of attaining that education. Educators must never lose sight of the goal or waver in our determination to provide all students with a truly empowering education. But in the face of inevitable student differences, we must also recognize that we need to adopt diverse pedagogical strategies in order to provide that best education for diverse children, including second-language learners of varying backgrounds. Sameness of treatment does not lead to equality of treatment. In fact, it nearly guarantees inequality by ignoring student differences.

Whenever I hear a teacher boast, "I treat all of my students alike," I know that this teacher has guaranteed inequality in educational opportunity—because students are not all alike. Students come to school speaking different languages. They bring varying home values and behavioral patterns. They have diverse learning styles. They have undergone different and sometimes soul-shattering experiences. They live in unequal socioeconomic conditions. Their prior education varies. They have different knowledge bases and experience-honed perspectives. They often lack self-esteem.

Many have little vision of future careers or awareness of what educational steps they must take in order to transform dreams into possibilities.

Group resource acculturation has at least two implications for reading instruction. First, reading teachers need to adapt their pedagogical strategies to student differences (Bilingual Education Office of the California Department of Education, 1986). Fortunately, the past two decades have brought considerable research on learning styles and human relations styles of students of different ethnic backgrounds. This research has also provided insights into how teachers can draw upon these differences as educational strengths (Hale-Benson, 1986; Ramírez & Castañeda, 1974; Vogt, Jordan, & Tharp, 1987).

Reading educators also have the opportunity of adding a second dimension of group resource acculturation to their instruction. Rather than simply recognizing cultural differences and adapting their instructional strategies, they can also contribute to building on those cultural variations in a way that both increases individual opportunities and adds to the richness of U.S. society.

A cogent example of the resources that can be used is the home languages that ESL learners bring to school. I am delighted that in my own state, California, the department of education has recognized home languages as a resource that should be developed. The 1989 *Foreign Language Framework* for kindergarten to grade 12 proclaims that education for the future must include education for language diversity combined with intercultural understanding (California Department of Education, 1989). First, it calls for continuous second-language education for all California students beginning in kindergarten and proceeding through grade 12. Second, it calls for that instruction to be communication based, with students learning to read, write, speak, and hear the language and not just to translate printed passages and take grammar examinations. Finally, it calls for California students to study language as a form of cultural expression by examining the culture or cultures from which it comes.

Moreover, in an enlightened recognition that individual opportunity and societal strength can be based on diversity as well as unity, the *Framework* recommends that California schools provide developmental K to 12 home-language education for all students who come from non-English-speaking homes or backgrounds. By addressing students' home language as a resource and strengthening it, schools can enhance individual and career opportunities and help students become more effective contributing citizens in a nation and world in which bilingual and multicultural skills will be both personal and societal assets. Note, for example, the tremendous opportunities in many parts of the world for fluently bilingual people in business, government, education, and the media, not to mention the constantly reported difficulties private and public institutions in the United States have in trying to fill bilingual positions.

Home-language group resource acculturation goes well beyond current transitional bilingual education, which generally uses home language and culture as tools for helping students to move into monocultural, English-language-only education. Rather it recognizes that students from non-English-speaking homes come to school with a special gift—introductory knowledge of other languages and cultures—and that schools should help empower students by developing those language skills rather than allowing them to languish.

In answer to those who argue that we should leave it to the home to develop those other languages, I respond that this simply is not a viable strategy. Homes do not teach language in the sense of developing the multiple skills of reading, writing, speaking, and hearing: they merely start children down the road of language development. Imagine, for example, what would happen to national literacy and language use if U.S. schools left the teaching of English to the home and decided not to teach English to monolingual English-speaking students!

The valuing and teaching of home languages has obvious implications for reading instruction, as reading would be an essential part of such language development. But what does it have to do with English-language reading education? Herein lies the second group resource acculturation contribution that English reading instruction can make. Reading teachers can select materials that broaden student knowledge of their own backgrounds and, more specifically, stories in English that dramatize the value of being bilingual. They can encourage students to develop their home languages, along with learning English, by emphasizing the personal and familial value of being bilingual and the expansion of career options that comes with full-scale bilingualism. Finally, they can work within their own institutions to create an atmosphere that encourages and implements multiple-language development.

Schools, in other words, should no longer encourage students to forget their home languages (or at least to put them on the academic back burner), to jettison their home cultures, and to plunge into a melting pot of cultural eradication. Rather, they should encourage the development of advanced bilingualism, in which English operates as the common societal language around which other languages can be arrayed. Many other nations have been providing multiple-language education for decades. The United States is long overdue in committing itself to catching up.

Civic Commitment Acculturation

The challenge of working toward civic commitment acculturation goes beyond knowledge, beyond skills, beyond understanding, and beyond sensitivity. It goes to the heart of civic dedication. Education for a future of societal multiethnicity and global interdependence demands civic commitment. In the words of Helen Keller, "Science may have found a cure for most evils; but it has found no remedy for the worst of them all—the apathy of human beings."

A 21st-century education should strive to help students become caring, not carefree. It should strive to help students become concerned about others as well as about themselves. It should strive to develop a sense of panhuman global identity that goes beyond—but does not supplant—familial, group, and national loyalties.

Once again, reading instruction can be on the front line of this quest for empowering civic commitment acculturation. First comes the selection of reading materials that offer role models for the importance of acting on civic virtues, particularly the importance of helping those within the students' own ethnic communities and reaching out to those of different backgrounds. Second comes the opportunity for teachers to engage students, including those who come from non-English-speaking homes (and often from nations with far different civic cultures), in an examination of what civic values and life can and should encompass in the United States.

Empowerment through Multiculturation

So there you have it: empowering multiculturation. Reading instruction for students of different cultural and linguistic backgrounds can foster such multiculturation by (1) expanding student knowledge of the United States, cultivating vital mainstream skills, and helping to develop English language facility; (2) exposing students to reading materials that increase understanding of U.S. societal diversity and insight into the cultures and experiences of Americans of different backgrounds; (3) employing instructional strategies that build on diverse student cultures and learning styles and using reading materials that encourage the maintenance of those cultural elements (such as home languages) that can enrich students' lives, expand career options, and prove of value to the nation; and (4) developing the intercultural civic virtues that can make the United States a better, more equitable place for all to live.

The challenge is tremendous, but the cost of failure is even greater. As England's Queen Victoria once admitted, "Change must be accepted...when it can no longer be resisted." In the face of multiethnic and global change, we must go beyond acceptance to careful thought and effective action. Reading instruction provides a natural and vital avenue for implementing multiculturation and empowering students from non-English-speaking homes. Playwright Samuel Beckett addressed that potential power when he wrote, "In reading, a voice comes to you and whispers, 'Imagine.'"

As we educate students for the 21st century, we must learn to draw selectively and effectively on *pluribus* and *unum,* on diversity and unity, as a basis for creating a better nation. It can be done. Whatever the obstacles, it must be done. As Pearl Buck once wrote, "All things are possible until they are proved impossible—and even the impossible may only be so as of now."

References

Bilingual Education Office of the California Department of Education. (1986). *Beyond language: Social and cultural factors in schooling language minority students.* Los Angeles, CA: California State University, Evaluation, Dissemination, and Assessment Center.

California Department of Education. (1989). *Foreign language framework.* Sacramento, CA: author.

Hale-Benson, J.E. (1986). *Black children: Their roots, culture, and learning styles* (rev. ed.). Baltimore, MD: Johns Hopkins University Press.

Ramírez, M., & Castañeda, A. (1974). *Cultural democracy: Bicognitive development and education.* New York: Academic.

Vogt, L.A., Jordan, C., & Tharp, R.G. (1987). Explaining school failure, producing school success: Two cases. *Anthropology and Education Quarterly, 18,* 276–286.

Jim Cummins

3

The Acquisition of English as a Second Language

There is general agreement among researchers in applied linguistics that acquisition of one's first language is an active process of construction in which one is driven by the need and desire to communicate. The same pattern is clearly evident among second-language learners in naturalistic contexts. However, variation both in rate of acquisition and in the ultimate level of proficiency attained is considerably more evident in second-language acquisition than in first (Wong Fillmore, 1991).

In this chapter I describe the sources of variation in second-language acquisition and draw out some of their implications for the teaching of English as a second language. First I clarify what is meant by "proficiency" in a language; in other words, what are the important dimensions of proficiency and how do they relate to one another? Second, I review research evidence on the length of time that is required to attain different aspects of proficiency in English as a second language. Then I examine the individual and situational factors that influence the rate of attainment and the ultimate level of proficiency in English as a second language and outline implications for program design for ESL teaching.

Dimensions of Language Proficiency

Appropriate ways of conceptualizing the nature of language proficiency and its relationship to other constructs (such as intelligence) have been debated by philosophers and psychologists since ancient times. However, the issue is not just an abstract theoretical question but one that is central to the resolution of a variety of applied educational issues. Educational policies are frequently based on assumptions about the nature of "language proficiency" and how long it takes to attain. For example, funding for English as a second language classes in the United States and Canada is based (at least in part) on assumptions about how long it takes immigrant students to acquire sufficient English proficiency to follow instruction in the regular classroom. Yet what exactly constitutes "English proficiency" is rarely analyzed by policymakers or researchers.

Misconceptions about the Nature of Language Proficiency

Two major misconceptions about the nature of language proficiency remain common among educators. These misconceptions have important practical implications for the way educators interact with ESL students. Both involve confusion between the surface or conversational aspects of children's language and the deeper aspects of proficiency that are more closely related to conceptual and academic development.

The first misconception entails drawing inferences about children's ability to think logically on the basis of their familiarity with and command of standard English. Children who speak a nonstandard variety of their first language (L1) are frequently thought to have a handicap in education and to be less capable of logical thinking. This assumption derives from the fact that the language of these children is viewed as inherently deficient as a tool for expressing logical relations. Since Labov's (1970) refutation of this position with respect to the language of African American inner-city children, it has had few adherents among applied linguists, although it is still a common misconception among educators and some academics who have little background in sociolinguistics.

A recent example of how persistent some of these linguistic prejudices are comes from a monograph on Hispanic children written by Dunn (1987), the primary author of the Peabody Picture Vocabulary Test. In expressing "traditionalists'" concerns that bilingual education could result in "at least the partial disintegration of the United States of America" (pp. 66–67), Dunn argues that "Latin pupils on the U.S. mainland, as a group, are inadequate bilinguals. They simply don't understand either English or Spanish well enough to function adequately in school" (p. 49). He goes on to argue that this is because most of these children "do not have the scholastic aptitude or linguistic ability to master two languages well, or to handle switching from one to the other, at school, as the language of instruction" (p. 71). He attributes the causes of this lower scholastic ability of Latino students more or less equally to environmental factors and to "genes that influence scholastic aptitude" (p. 64). (See the special issue of the *Hispanic Journal of Behavioral Science,* Volume 10, 1988, for critical discussion of Dunn's views.)

The second misconception is in many respects the converse of the first. In this case, ESL students' adequate control over the surface features of English (that is, their ability to converse fluently in English) is taken as an indication that all aspects of their "English proficiency" have been mastered to the same extent as that demonstrated by native speakers of the language. In other words, conversational skills are interpreted as a valid index of overall language proficiency.

This process has been documented in the psychological assessment of ESL students (Cummins, 1984). When such students experience academic difficulties, educators frequently wonder whether they have some form of learning disability or whether the difficulties are simply a function of the fact that they still have an inadequate grasp of

English. Such ESL students may appear to have overcome difficulties in English since they frequently understand and speak English relatively well. However, when tested by IQ and other psychological tests in English they often score much lower on the verbal than on the performance subtests. This has led many students to be labeled as "learning disabled" and given a one-way ticket into special education classes. Ortiz and Yates (1983), for example, report that Latino students in Texas were overrepresented in the "learning disability" category by more than 300 percent.

Once again, the problem is directly related to the way in which language proficiency has been conceptualized: specifically, students' conversational fluency in English is taken as a valid reflection of their overall proficiency in the language. Furthermore, it is assumed that because students can converse adequately in English, their English proficiency is sufficient to ensure that verbal IQ tests do not discriminate against them on the basis of language; in other words, psychologists erroneously view the test as measuring academic potential rather than present level of academic functioning in English.

In the case of both of these misconceptions, a close relationship is assumed between the two faces of language proficiency, the conversational and the academic. In order to address these misconceptions and clarify the relationship between language proficiency and minority students' academic progress, I have suggested that it is necessary to make a fundamental distinction between conversational and academic aspects of language proficiency (Cummins, 1984). This distinction is similar to that proposed by a number of other investigators (see, for example, Bruner, 1975; Donaldson, 1978; Olson, 1977). These investigators have pointed to a distinction between contextualized and decontextualized language as fundamental to understanding the nature of children's language and literacy development. The terms used by different investigators vary, but they all emphasize the extent to which the meaning being communicated is supported by contextual cues (such as gestural and intonation cues present in face-to-face interaction) or dependent largely on linguistic cues that are largely independent of the immediate communicative context. To illustrate: in written text, a cohesive device such as *however* at the beginning of a sentence tells the proficient reader to expect some qualification of the statement that immediately precedes it.

In discussing this distinction between contextualized and decontextualized language, I originally used the terms *basic interpersonal communicative skills* (BICS) and *cognitive academic language proficiency* (CALP) and later (see, for example, Cummins, 1984) elaborated the distinction into a framework that distinguishes among the cognitive and contextual demands made by particular forms of communication.

Cognitive and Contextual Demands

The framework outlined in Figure 1 is designed to identify the extent to which ESL students are able to cope successfully with the cognitive and linguistic demands made on them by the social and educational environment in which they are obliged to function. These dimensions are conceptualized within a framework made up of the intersection of two continua, one relating to the range of contextual support available for expressing or receiving meaning and the other relating to the amount of information that must be processed simultaneously or in close succession by the student in order to carry out the activity.

In the context-embedded–context-reduced continuum its extremes are distinguished by the fact that in context-embedded communication the participants can actively negotiate meaning (by indicating when a message has not been understood, for example) and the language use is supported by a range of meaningful interpersonal and situational cues. Context-reduced communication, on the other hand, relies on linguistic cues to meaning; thus, the successful interpretation of the message depends heavily on knowledge of the language itself. In general, context-embedded

Figure 1
Range of Contextual Support and Degree of Cognitive Involvement in Communicative Activities

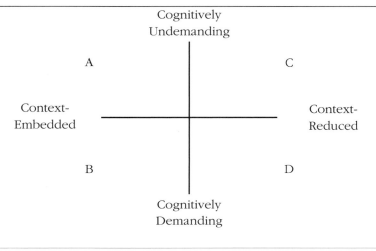

communication is more typical of the everyday world outside the classroom, whereas many of the linguistic demands of the classroom reflect communicative activities that are at the context-reduced end of the continuum. The upper parts of the vertical continuum consist of communicative tasks and activities that require linguistic tools whose use has become largely automatic; these tasks, therefore, require little active cognitive involvement for appropriate performance. At the lower end of the continuum are tasks and activities that require active cognitive involvement.

The framework elaborates on the conversational-academic (or BICS-CALP) distinction by highlighting important underlying dimensions of conversational and academic communication. Persuading another individual that your point of view is correct and writing an essay are examples of quadrant B and D skills respectively. Quadrant A skills such as conversational abilities often develop relatively quickly among ESL students because these forms of communication are supported by interpersonal and contextual cues and make relatively few cognitive demands on the individual. Mastery of the academic functions of language found in quadrant D, on the other hand, is a more formidable task because such activities require high levels of cognitive involvement and are minimally supported by contextual or interpersonal cues.

It is important to stress that the distinction between conversational aspects and academic aspects of language proficiency is not one between oral and written language. Performing an oral cloze task may be far more context reduced than sending an electronic mail message to a good friend, an activity that in many respects is highly context embedded.

How Long Does It Take ESL Students to Master Different Aspects of Proficiency?

One application of the framework shown in Figure 1 is in the interpretation of data regarding the length of time required for ESL students to develop proficiency in different aspects of English. Two large-scale studies have reported that, on average, at least five years is required for ESL students to attain grade norms on academic (context-reduced, cognitively demanding) aspects of English proficiency (Collier, 1987, 1989; Cummins, 1981). Collier's data suggest that ESL students born in the United States or arriving there at an early age are in a somewhat worse situation in that they require, on average, seven years of schooling to catch up academically with their native-English-speaking peers. Other research suggests that a much shorter period (fewer than two years) is usually required for immigrant students to attain age-appropriate levels of proficiency in conversational (context-embedded, cognitively undemanding) aspects of their second language (see, for example, Gonzalez, 1986; Snow & Hoefnagel-Hohle, 1978). These patterns are depicted in Figure 2.

There are two reasons that such major differences are found in the length of time required to attain age-appropriate levels of conversational and academic skills.

Figure 2
Length of Time Required to
Achieve Age-Appropriate Levels of
Conversational and Academic Communicative Proficiency

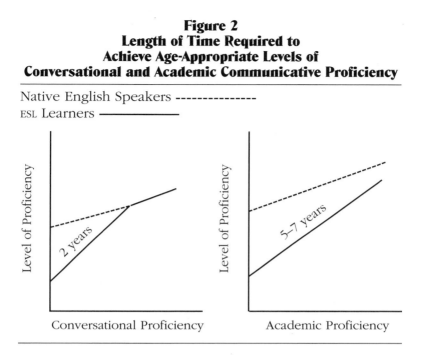

Native English Speakers -------------
ESL Learners ——————

First, as outlined above, considerably less knowledge of language per se is usually required to function appropriately in interpersonal communicative situations than in academic situations. The social expectations of the learner and sensitivity to paralinguistic and contextual cues greatly facilitate communication of meaning. These cues are largely absent in academic situations such as reading a social studies text. The second reason is that native English speakers do not stand still, waiting for ESL students to catch up. A major goal of schooling for all children is to expand their ability to manipulate language in increasingly decontextualized situations, and every year native-English-speaking students gain more sophisticated vocabulary and grammatical knowledge and increase their literacy skills. Thus, ESL students must catch up with a moving target, and it is not surprising that this formidable task is seldom complete in one or two years. By contrast, in the area of conversational skills, most native speakers reach a plateau relatively early in schooling: a typical six-year-old can express herself as adequately as an older child on most of the topics she is likely to speak on and can understand most of what is likely to be said to her. While some increase in sophistication can be expected with increasing age, the differences are not particularly salient in comparison to differences in other literacy-related skills.

One further point should be addressed with respect to the influence of age on English acquisition. The research data suggest that immigrant children who arrive in a new country at different ages approach grade norms in English academic skills at approximately the same rate (Cummins, 1981). What this implies is that older children make more rapid progress in absolute terms than do younger children. Expressed differently, a child who arrives in the United States or Canada at age 12 will have acquired more English academic skills in absolute terms after 1 year than her 8-year-old sister, despite the fact that they may be equally behind their respective grade norms.

The trends depicted in this section have immediate relevance for two practical issues. First, they show that ESL support is still beneficial (and frequently necessary) even after students have attained conversational fluency in English. Exiting children prematurely from ESL or bilingual support programs may jeopardize their academic development, particularly if the mainstream classroom does not provide an environment that is supportive of language acquisition. It is also clear that psychoeducational assessment of ESL students is likely to underestimate their academic potential to a significant extent if any credence is placed in the test norms, which are derived predominantly from native-English-speaking students. In a 1984 study, for example, I found that typical verbal IQ tests underestimate the academic potential of ESL students who had been in Canadian or U.S. schools for 3 years by a factor of 15 points. As the numbers of ESL students increase, a radical restructuring of special education assessment and provision will be required (Rueda, 1989).

Although the average trends depicted here appear to be reliably established at this point, there are major individual differences in the rate of acquisition and level of ultimate attainment in both conversational and academic aspects of English among ESL students. In the next section, two frameworks for conceptualizing variations in acquisition of English as a second language—those of Cummins (1981) and Wong Fillmore (1991)—are integrated to provide a picture of the complex interactions at work in this process.

Understanding Individual Differences in English Acquisition

Krashen (1989) has suggested that the major causal variable in second-language acquisition is the amount of *comprehensible input* the learner receives. In other words, exposure to the target language in itself is insufficient for acquisition to occur; it must be exposure that the learner can and is motivated to make sense of. The term *comprehensible input* has the advantage of highlighting the fact that two very different components must be included in discussions of second-language acquisition: the nature of the target-language input itself and the attributes of the individual that determine her or his ability and inclination to make sense of the input.

But the term also has a disadvantage. It suggests that language learning is largely a passive process of receiving input (although Krashen himself has always emphasized the active constructive nature of the process of comprehension). There is some consensus among applied linguists that *active* use of the target language also plays an extremely important role in the acquisition process. Thus, it seems reasonable to emphasize *communicative interaction* and the negotiation of meaning between learners and competent users of the target language as central to the second language acquisition process. Communicative interaction incorporates the notion of comprehensible input but also highlights the importance of active use of oral and written language for optimal acquisition to occur (Swain, 1986). It should be noted that communicative interaction refers not just to the negotiation of meaning through conversation but also to engagement with written texts, which serve crucial roles as both input and output for ESL learners in academic contexts.

Figure 3 suggests that quantity and quality of input directly affect the amount of comprehensible input that learners receive and the amount of comprehensible output (in Swain's terms) they send. Together, comprehensible input and output constitute the quantity and quality of communicative interaction (in both oral and written modes) that the learner engages in. This is seen as a direct determinant of the development of second-language proficiency. Also shown in Figure 3 is the influence of learner attributes. Attributes interact with input to determine what will actually be understood. For example, a child with a high level of conceptual development in her first language has more cognitive power to make sense of the input than one who has a less well-developed conceptual foundation. Attributes also affect the extent to which learners actually use the language (output). For example, a highly sociable child is likely to seek out interaction with native speakers to a greater extent than one who is shy. The sociable child is likely to get more comprehensible input as a result of his interactional style.

A centrally important attribute of the learner, one that is more amenable to teacher influence than either personality or cognitive ability, is the extent to which the learners have confidence in their identity and ability to learn. One way of conceptualizing this attribute is in terms of the degree to which ESL learners feel empowered in the learning situation (Cummins, 1989). When school personnel reject students' identities (by punishing them for using their native language, for example), they force students to make an unnecessary and potentially traumatic choice between their two cultures, and the resulting conflict may actually

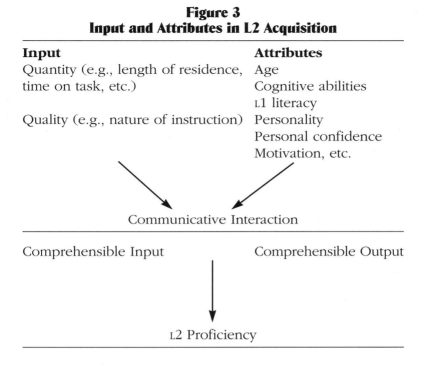

Figure 3
Input and Attributes in L2 Acquisition

Input	**Attributes**
Quantity (e.g., length of residence, time on task, etc.)	Age
	Cognitive abilities
	L1 literacy
Quality (e.g., nature of instruction)	Personality
	Personal confidence
	Motivation, etc.

Communicative Interaction

Comprehensible Input   Comprehensible Output

L2 Proficiency

interfere with language learning. Similarly, instruction that students are unable to relate to their previous experiences fails to validate those experiences. In short, students vary in the level of self-confidence they bring to the language-learning situation, but the level is also significantly affected by the extent to which experiences in the language-learning situation encourage them to actively use language to express and share their identity. Enright and McCloskey (1988) suggest that "as teachers we only fool ourselves if we think we can teach language skills or literacy without integrating students' own ideas, purposes and dreams into the teaching program" (p. 10). If the ideas, purposes and dreams of ESL students are denied expression in the classroom, those students are unlikely to feel a sense of belonging or community within the school environment, which for them provides their initial and probably most formative experience of their new society.

The nature of the input may also influence the amount and quality of the language learners use—that is, their comprehensible output. For example, learners use far less of the new or "target" language (TL) in classrooms that are highly teacher centered—where the teacher does most of the talking—than in classrooms that are more project oriented—where students are actively engaged in using language to solve problems or carry out research. The former classroom may provide an appropriate environment for students at early stages of the acquisition process (provided the teacher's language is at an appropriate level for the learners to understand), but at later stages active oral- and written-language use is important if proficiency is to continue developing.

Wong Fillmore's (1991) model provides a more detailed treatment of the attribute- and input-based sources of variation in second-language acquisition. There are three major components to the model: (1) learners who realize they need to speak TL and are motivated to do so; (2) TL speakers who know the language well enough to provide the learners with access to it and to reinforce the need for learning it; and (3) a social setting that brings learners and TL speakers into sufficiently frequent contact to make language learning possible.

In addition to these three basic components, there are three interconnected processes that come into play in language learning: social, linguistic, and cognitive. The *social processes* refer to the steps taken cooperatively by learners and TL speakers to create a social setting in which they desire to communicate by means of the target language. In these settings, learners make use of their knowledge to figure out what people might be saying, given the social situation. Furthermore, Wong Fillmore points out the following:

Those situations that promote frequent contacts are the best, especially if the contacts last long enough to give learners ample opportunity to observe people using the language for a variety of communicative purposes. Those which also permit learners to engage in the frequent use of the language with speakers are even better (1991, p. 54).

Linguistic processes refer to the assumptions held by TL speakers and learners that cause them to produce or interpret linguistic data in ways that promote communication. Linguistic data derived from a supportive social context allow learners to discover how the language works and is used. As a result of their first language competence, learners are able to make educated guesses about what TL speakers are likely to talk about in a variety of situations. This transfer process can have both positive and negative consequences, but on the whole, according to Wong Fillmore, the outcomes of transfer are positive:

Because they already have a language, they know about linguistic categories such as lexical item, clause, and phrase. This awareness of grammatical form and structures will predispose them to look for equivalent properties in the new language data that they have available to them. Similarly, through the experiences they have had in their first language, learners are generally knowledgeable about the speech acts and functions that can be performed linguistically. . . . The assumption that forms will be found in the L2 [second language], which are functionally equivalent to L1 [first language] forms, can lead learners to acquire them more efficiently than they might otherwise. At the same time, however, it can also interfere with learning, since this assumption sometimes leads learners to draw largely unwarranted conclusions that L2 forms are structurally and functionally identical to L1 forms and usages (1991, pp. 55–56).

Finally, *cognitive processes* in language learning "involve the analytical procedures and operations that take place in the heads of learners and ultimately result in the acquisition of the language" (Wong Fillmore, 1991, p. 56). Learners use cognitive processes such as memory, categorization, generalization, and inference to discover the system of rules that TL speakers follow, synthesize these rules into a grammar, and then internalize it such that they can use it for producing their own semantically and syntactically appropriate utterances.

Among the sources of variation in learner characteristics, Wong Fillmore lists cognitive abilities, age, and personality (for example, mental rigidity, or propensity for risk taking). The results of a study carried out by Cummins et al. (1984) suggest that these variables may be differentially related to various aspects of proficiency, with personality variables being more related to interactional style in conversation and cognitive variables more related to the development of academic abilities in the L2.

Age clearly contributes to the cognitive power of the learner (at least up to adolescence) in that older learners are more cognitively mature than younger learners. A considerable number of studies have shown that older learners are more efficient in second-language learning, although their ultimate attainment in the language may not surpass that of younger learners who have more time to develop proficiency (see, for example, Krashen, Long, & Scarcella, 1979). Wong Fillmore also points out that the cognitive advantages that come with age and experience do not always result in better language learning for older learners because social and communicative needs become more complex with increasing age and can interfere with the process.

One important additional contributor to the learners' cognitive power is the degree of literacy developed in the first language. There is considerable evidence of interdependence of literacy-related or academic skills across languages (see, for example, Cummins, 1984), such that the better developed the conceptual foundation of children's first language, the more likely children are to develop similarly high levels of conceptual abilities in their second language. This interdependence of academic aspects of proficiency across languages has been used to explain the fact that in bilingual programs, instruction in a minority language results in no academic loss in the majority language for either minority or majority students. In fact, an inverse relationship between amount of instruction in English and English academic achievement is frequently observed for minority students. For example, Ramirez, Yuen, and Ramey (1991) reported from a large-scale longitudinal study that Latino students who had received at least 40 percent of their instruction in Spanish throughout elementary school appeared to have better prospects of catching up academically in English with their native-English-speaking peers than did Latino students who had received all their instruction in English or who had been exited to an all-English program in the early grades.

With respect to variation in social settings, Wong Fillmore points out that they work best for language learning when TL speakers outnumber learners and when they are structured in ways that maximize interaction between the two groups. *Direct* interaction between learners and TL speakers may not be absolutely necessary for learning to take place: some learners appear to be able to pick up the TL simply by observing teachers and peers. According to Wong Fillmore, this can happen when the setting offers access to meaningful input and opportunities to practice the language in the context of structured activities: "It appears that what is essential is that learners have access to language that is appropriately modified for them, and is used in ways that allow learners to discover its formal and pragmatic properties" (1991, p. 64). Thus, access to communicative interaction is crucial, although the learner may not necessarily have to participate directly in the interaction.

Variation in the behavior, attitudes, and beliefs of TL speakers (including teachers) will also affect the extent to which learners can get access to sufficient linguistic data to learn the language. For example, TL speakers who believe that TL learners will not comprehend natural uses of the language may make inappropriate adjustments in their speech, whereas others may believe that adjustments are unnecessary and go on to speak in ways that are incomprehensible to the learners. This situation may be particularly prevalent in high school content classes where teachers have little formal training in issues related to ESL learners. Students who have developed conversational skills in English may appear fully competent, and their teachers consequently may make few, if any adjustments in their use of English or in their expectations regarding the quality of the English used by students in assignments. There may be little attempt to integrate the teaching of content and language in these settings so that neither content nor language gets learned particularly well (Early, 1990; Mohan, 1986).

These variations in TL speakers' behavior and in social settings can dramatically affect the amount of language children learn. For example, in one of the classrooms observed by Wong Fillmore, 40 percent of the children who entered school at the beginning of the year had learned no English by the end of it, regardless of whether they were shy and socially inept or outgoing and socially skilled. The teacher and her assistant used English exclusively, but there were few teacher-directed instructional activities or instances of formal instruction over the course of the year. Teachers monitored children's self-selected activities closely and interacted with them on an individual basis, but these opportunities for children to hear and learn English were not frequent enough for most of the learners to sustain language-learning efforts.

Implications for Teaching ESL Students

Clearly there is immense variation in learner attributes and in the quality and quantity of input TL speakers provide to learners in particular social settings. This variation directly affects the communicative interaction that learners can observe or participate in. Although teachers may have limited power to affect most learner attributes, they can modify their own behavior, both as providers of TL input and as organizers of social settings in which learners feel sufficiently confident to engage in active use of the TL.

Despite the variation that characterizes the ESL learning process, there are certain principles that can guide the provision and organization of learning settings for ESL students. The principles (adapted from Ashworth, Cummins, & Handscombe, 1989) outlined in what follows summarize the points made earlier in the paper and draw out their implications for the teaching situation.

1. *The educational and personal experiences that ESL students bring to schools constitute the foundation for all their future learning; schools should therefore attempt to amplify rather than replace these experiences.*

Schools communicate subtle (and sometimes not-so-subtle) messages to ESL students regarding the value of their prior experiences and the appropriateness of their language and culture within the context of their new country. Research suggests that students who are valued by the wider society (and by the schools that inevitably tend to reflect that society) succeed to a greater extent than students whose backgrounds are devalued (see, for example, Ogbu, 1978).

Students' cultural identities are likely to be validated by instructional programs that attempt to add English to the languages that students bring to school while encouraging them to continue developing their first-language skills. On the other hand, programs that attempt to replace students' first language with English may undermine the self-confidence that is essential to students' academic progress. In addition, the conceptual knowledge that students possess in their first language constitutes a major component of the cognitive power that they bring to the language-learning situation. It thus makes sense to value and, where possible, continue to cultivate these abilities, both for their own sake and to facilitate transfer to the TL.

2. *Although English conversational skills may be acquired quite rapidly by ESL students, upward of five years may be required for ESL students to reach a level of academic proficiency in English comparable to their native-English-speaking peers; schools must therefore be prepared to make a long-term commitment to supporting the academic development of ESL students.*

There are several implications of the different time periods required to develop age-appropriate levels of conversational and academic skills. First, it is clearly not sufficient to get students over the initial difficulties of acquiring English. Progress must be monitored for several years after students appear to be comfortable in English to ensure that they are coping with and acquiring an ability to manipulate the more formal, impersonal, and abstract language that becomes increasingly important for school success in upper grades.

Another implication is that ESL should not be a separate program that exists apart from the mainstream of the educational system. Withdrawal of ESL students from the regular classroom may sometimes be necessary and appropriate in the early stages of learning, but it is not a viable option over the length of time that students may need support in mastering the academic aspects of English. Thus, it is likely that all teachers in a school will be required to address the needs of ESL students by individualizing instruction to take account of different levels of English proficiency and different rates of learning.

3. *Access to interaction with English speakers is a major causal variable underlying both the acquisition of English and ESL students' sense of belonging to the English-speaking society; the entire school is therefore responsible for supporting the learning and need for interaction of ESL students, and ESL provision should integrate students into the social and academic mainstream to whatever extent possible.*

Enright and McCloskey (1988) have quite clearly expressed the importance of genuine interaction in the classroom and the relationship between this point and the first principle outlined in the preceding paragraphs:

> Students fully develop second language and literacy through using the second language in many different settings, with a wide variety of respondents and audiences (including themselves) and for a wide variety of purposes. . . . Students' language and literacy development is facilitated by a comfortable atmosphere: one that values, encourages and celebrates efforts to use language; that focuses primarily on the meaning and intention of utterances and messages rather than on their form; and that treats "errors" as a normal part of becoming increasingly better thinkers and communicators (1988, p. 21).

It is important to emphasize that a focus on promoting interaction with native speakers certainly does not imply placement of ESL students into regular classrooms without provision of additional support for both students and their teachers. Nor does it imply a pull-out program that offers support in a segregated setting for part of the day and mainstreaming for the rest. What tends to happen in the latter case is that students flounder in the mainstreamed part of the day because no support is provided in those classes. At the same time, both teacher and student tend to assume that the short period of pull-out assistance is the only learning for the day and the rest of the day is spent marking time until increased proficiency is acquired through the language program.

What is required is the provision of instructional strategies within the mainstreamed classroom that are appropriate for all students—peer tutoring, cooperative learning, creative writing, and project-oriented activities. Such activities are effective for academic and language development as well as for intercultural understanding. A frequently neglected aspect of culturally and linguistically diverse classrooms is the opportunity they provide to teachers to explore curricular topics from many different cultural perspectives. By recognizing diversity as a valuable resource, teachers not only validate the cultural backgrounds of ESL students but also offer all students valuable possibilities for cultural enrichment.

4. *If ESL students are to catch up academically with their native-English-speaking peers, their cognitive growth and mastery of academic content must continue while English is being learned. Thus, the teaching of English as a second language should be integrated with the teaching of other academic content that is appropriate to students' cognitive level. By the same token, all content teachers must recognize themselves also as teachers of language.*

As discussed previously, language learning is a process that takes time; ESL students may require five (or more) years to catch up with their native English-speaking peers in academic aspects of English. Clearly, ESL students' cognitive growth and their learning of subject matter content cannot be postponed until their English-language skills are developed to the level of their classmates'. In recognition of this reality, educators have increasingly emphasized the importance of integrating language teaching with the teaching of academic content. Effective instruction—whether in mainstreamed or pull-out classes—simultaneously promotes language, cognition, and content mastery. In the absence of this integration, the already formidable task that ESL students face in catching up to their native-English-speaking peers will be rendered considerably more difficult.

The modifications to the instructional program required to integrate language and content in a manner appropriate for ESL students do not entail a dilution in the conceptual or academic content of the instruction but rather require the adoption of instructional strategies that take account of students' academic backgrounds and ensure comprehension of the material being presented. One such strategy emphasized by Mohan (1986) and Early (1990) is the use of "key visuals" (diagrams, graphs, timelines, etc.)

as a means of adapting content for ESL learners and making new information at least partially understandable.

In short, content-based language instruction is particularly appropriate to address the learning needs of ESL students and help them bridge the linguistic and academic gap between themselves and students who are native English speakers.

5. *The academic and linguistic growth of ESL students is significantly increased when their parents see themselves and are seen by school staff as coeducators of their children. Schools should therefore actively seek to establish a collaborative relationship with parents of ESL students that encourages them to participate in furthering their children's academic progress.*

The most clear-cut evidence of the academic benefits that can accrue to ESL students as a result of the establishment of a collaborative relationship between the school and parents is found in a two-year experiment conducted in the borough of Haringey, a working-class area of London, England, by Tizard, Schofield, and Hewison (1982). The experiment consisted of having parents listen on a regular basis to their children read books sent home from school. These children's reading progress was compared to that of children who were given additional reading instruction in small groups several times a week by a trained reading specialist. Many parents in the district spoke little or no English and many were illiterate in both English and their first language (Greek and Bengali, for the most part). Despite these factors, parents, almost without exception, welcomed the project and agreed to listen to their children read as requested and to complete a record card showing what had been read.

The researchers found that children who read to their parents made significantly greater progress in reading than those who were given additional reading instruction, and this was particularly so for children who, at the beginning of the project, were experiencing difficulty learning to read. In addition, most parents expressed great satisfaction at being involved in this way by the schools, and teachers reported that the children showed an increased interest in school learning and were better behaved. Lack of literacy or English fluency did not detract from parents' willingness to collaborate with the school, nor did it prevent improvement in these children's reading.

In general, successful parental involvement is likely to depend on the extent to which parents see the school as welcoming rather than as the intimidating environment it often is for many parents with limited knowledge of English. Clearly, the presence in the school of staff who speak the language of the parents will greatly facilitate parental involvement (Ramirez, Yuen, & Ramey, 1991).

In addition to the family literacy project investigated by Tizard, Schofield, and Hewison, there are many other possibilities for encouraging parental involvement: having students carry out research on their family's social history through interviewing parents, grandparents, and other relatives, for example (see Lopes & Lopes, 1991), or getting parents and children to collaborate in writing projects (see Ada, 1988).

Expanding Horizons

Demographic changes in North America and elsewhere have brought educational and social issues related to language learning to the forefront of public discussion. While many questions remain, a considerable body of research and theory has accumulated to guide policy and practice. We know, for example, that there are complex interactions between the attributes the learner brings to the language learning situation and the input that speakers of the target language provide in particular social settings. Learner attributes may differ in their importance for acquiring proficiency in different aspects of the TL; for example, level of cognitive maturity and first-language literacy may be more important for development of academic (as compared to conversational) aspects of proficiency, whereas the opposite may be true for personality variables that influence learners' inclination to actively engage in interpersonal exchanges with native speakers.

Access to communicative interaction in which the learner can gather linguistic data is viewed by most theorists as a central factor in the language-acquisition process. This principle carries important implications for the organization of learning within schools. For example, it implies that students should have access to competent users of the TL and engage in academic activities with them that stimulate language acquisition, literacy development, and critical-thinking abilities. This implies both greater integration of language and content teaching than has been the case in many mainstreamed classrooms and also encouragement of active use of written and oral language by students. This latter point becomes especially important in view of the fact that ESL students are likely to be behind their native-English-speaking peers in English academic abilities for several years and only active use of the language will enable them to deepen their conceptual foundation in English and transfer what they already know in their first language to their second.

Finally and probably most important, ESL students do not come to the task of learning English as blank slates. Their cultural identity and first-language abilities provide the personal and academic foundation for growth in English and integration into a new society. What the student brings to the classroom should ideally be treated by the teacher as a resource, not just for the student's own learning but also for the enrichment of instruction for all students, whether fluent speakers of English or learners of English. By the same token, parents of ESL students are potential resources both for their own children and for the school as a whole. When the school establishes genuine partnerships with parents, both they and their children have the potential to bring a breadth of education to the monolingual English-speaking child who might otherwise be limited to just one narrow cultural perspective on an increasingly interdependent global society.

Author's note: I would like to thank Lily Wong Fillmore for many discussions on several of the ideas developed in this chapter. I would also like to acknowledge the contributions of Mary Ashworth and Jean Handscombe, with whom the principles outlined in the second part of the chapter were developed collaboratively in the context of carrying out a review of the Vancouver School Board's ESL program.

References

Ada, A.F. (1988). The Pajaro Valley experience: Working with Spanish-speaking parents to develop children's reading and writing skills in the home through the use of children's literature. In T. Skutnabb-Kangas & J. Cummins (Eds.), *Minority education: From shame to struggle* (pp. 223–238). Clevedon, UK: Multilingual Matters.

Ashworth, M., Cummins, J., & Handscombe, J. (1989, January). *Report on the Vancouver School Board's ESL program*. Report submitted to the Vancouver School Board, British Columbia.

Bruner, J.S. (1975). Language as an instrument of thought. In A. Davies (Ed.) *Problems of language and learning*. London: Heinemann.

Collier, V.P. (1987). Age and rate of acquisition of second language for academic purposes. *TESOL Quarterly, 21,* 617–641.

Collier, V.P. (1989). How long? A synthesis of research on academic achievement in a second language. *TESOL Quarterly, 23,* 509–631.

Cummins, J. (1981). Age on arrival and immigrant second language learning in Canada: A reassessment. *Applied Linguistics, 2,* 132–149.

Cummins, J. (1984). *Bilingualism and special education: Issues in assessment and pedagogy*. Clevedon, UK: Multilingual Matters.

Cummins, J. (1989). *Empowering minority students*. Sacramento, CA: California Association for Bilingual Education.

Cummins, J., Swain, M., Nakajima, K., Handscombe, J., Green, D., & Tran, C. (1984). Linguistic interdependence among Japanese and Vietnamese immigrant students. In C. Rivera (Ed.), *Communicative competence approaches to language proficiency assessment: Research and application*. Clevedon, UK: Multilingual Matters.

Donaldson, M. (1978). *Children's minds*. Glasgow, UK: Collins.

Dunn, L. (1987). *Bilingual Hispanic children on the U.S. mainland: A review of research on their cognitive, linguistic, and scholastic development*. Circle Pines, MN: American Guidance Service.

Early, M. (1990). Enabling first and second language learners in the classroom. *Language Arts, 67,* 567–575.

Enright, D.S., & McCloskey, M.L. (1988). *Integrating English: Developing English language and literacy in the multilingual classroom.* Reading, MA: Addison-Wesley.

Gonzalez, L.A. (1986). *The effects of first language education on the second language and academic achievement of Mexican immigrant elementary school children in the United States.* Unpublished doctoral dissertation, University of Illinois at Urbana–Champaign.

Krashen, S. (1989). *Language acquisition and language education.* Englewood Cliffs, NJ: Prentice Hall.

Krashen, S., Long, M., & Scarcella, R. (1979). Age, rate and eventual attainment in second language acquisition. *TESOL Quarterly, 13,* 573–582.

Labov, W. (1970). *The logic of non-standard English.* Urbana, IL: National Council of Teachers of English.

Lopes, J., & Lopes, M. (1991). Bridging the generation gap: The collection of social histories in the Portuguese Heritage Language Program. *The Canadian Modern Language Review, 47,* 708–711.

Mohan, B.A. (1986). *Language and content.* Reading, MA: Addison-Wesley.

Ogbu, J. (1978). *Minority education and caste.* New York: Academic.

Olson, D.R. (1977). From utterance to text: The bias of language in speech and writing. *Harvard Educational Review, 47,* 257–281.

Ortiz, A.A., & Yates, J.R. (1983). Incidence of exceptionality among Hispanics: Implications for manpower planning. *NABE Journal, 7,* 41–54.

Ramirez, J.D., Yuen, S.D., & Ramey, D.R. (1991). *Executive summary—final report: Longitudinal study of structured English immersion strategy, early-exit and late-exit transitional bilingual education programs for language-minority children* (Contract No. 300-87-0156, submitted to the U.S. Department of Education). San Mateo, CA: Aguirre International.

Rueda, R. (1989). Defining mild disabilities with language-minority students. *Exceptional Children, 56,* 121–128.

Snow, D.E., & Hoefnagel-Hohle, M. (1978). The critical period for language acquisition: Evidence from second language learning. *Child Development, 49,* 1114–1128.

The Acquisition of English as a Second Language   **61**

Swain, M. (1986). Communicative competence: Some roles of comprehensible input and comprehensible output in its development. In J. Cummins & M. Swain, (Eds.), *Bilingualism in education: Aspects of theory, research and practice.* London: Longman.

Tizard, J., Schofield, W.N., & Hewison, J. (1982). Collaboration between teachers and parents in assisting children's reading. *British Journal of Educational Psychology, 52,* 1–15.

Wong Fillmore, L. (1991). Second-language learning in children: A model of language learning in social context. In E. Bialystok (Ed.) *Language processing in bilingual children* (pp. 49–69). Cambridge, UK: Cambridge University Press.

Section 2

Organizing for Instruction

When organizing for instruction there are many factors that need to be considered. The chapters in this section highlight what we believe are the most important of these factors: promoting self-esteem, implementing instructional approaches and teaching procedures, and identifying materials needed to enhance instruction.

Chapter 4 addresses the role of student self-esteem in accessing literacy in multicultural and multilingual classrooms. Although teachers typically deal with the issue of self-esteem at the individual-student level, we believe that everyone must be aware of and sensitive to the social and political contexts in which self-esteem is developed and nurtured in general terms in the classroom. Only when we have recognized this broader perspective can we help students achieve their greatest potential.

There is a wide range of abilities and needs in every classroom in every school. For this reason, no single method, strategy, or approach is appropriate for every learner or teacher. In recognition of these differences in learning and teaching styles, chapter 5 presents a variety of instructional procedures and approaches for teachers to consider.

Due to the ever-increasing diversity of the student population, the identification, development, and provision of appropriate instructional materials pose challenges. Far too frequently the special needs of ESL students are overlooked when materials are selected, resulting in a mismatch between the materials and the cultural and linguistic backgrounds of the learners. Chapter 6 provides a list of criteria for selecting reading materials for ESL students, as well as suggestions for materials that meet those criteria.

of respect, and encourages pride in self, language, and culture. In order to develop a curriculum capable of supporting self-esteem in ESL students, we must adopt a social and political perspective. Though self-esteem may be manifested at the level of the individual student, it is the social and political context of the classroom that offers the most powerful means of understanding and addressing the problem of nurturing it.

The social context of the classroom affects the language learning of students acquiring English, in that language is clearly learned, adapted, and created within a social setting. Along with the structural rules of the language, language learners internalize the social roles and relationships inherent in communication. When self-esteem is understood as the preservation of one's dignity in relationship to others, it becomes quite evident that careful examination of the social context surrounding the classroom language learning of ESL students holds great potential.

Political factors related to the issue of self-esteem, though perhaps less obvious, are no less powerful than the social factors. It has long been suggested that classrooms reflect and maintain the political structure of the society, including inequities in relation to race, sex, language, and class (Apple, 1982; Giroux, 1983; McDermott, 1987). In classrooms, these inequalities can be manifested in terms of unequal levels of student dominance and participation in the everyday social and linguistic events related to learning. There are those whose language, culture, and knowledge are accepted and affirmed and whose sense of dignity and self-worth is thereby nurtured. For those whose language, culture, and knowledge do not reflect the dominant society, however, schooling can be a denigrating experience. Giroux asserts that schools can resist this reality, but resistance can only occur through conscious awareness on the part of all participants in the learning environment. We believe that addressing the issue of self-esteem for ESL students necessitates recognition of the inherently political nature of schooling as it is manifested in the language-learning environment of the classroom. Teachers who want all students, including those learning English as a second language, to participate fully in academic endeavors and eventually to lead productive and satisfying lives must establish a social and political classroom context that builds students' feelings of self-worth and dignity.

As far as literacy learning for ESL students is concerned, self-esteem must be understood as a matter of access—that is, as the right to full participation in and ownership of literacy events. The time it takes to develop English language proficiency may vary from student to student (Collier, 1987; Cummins, 1981), but the right to access cannot be denied or delayed until proficiency is achieved. Teachers must provide all students with access to meaningful and purposeful literacy events in the classroom throughout the school day. Students must develop a personal sense of power over written language, the confidence to take risks, and the willingness to construct their own meanings. It is through access to literacy that ESL students' self-esteem is developed and preserved.

In this chapter, we outline a framework for understanding and addressing the issue of self-esteem for ESL students in relationship to literacy development and instruction. We offer our concept of a classroom that supports and encourages the literacy development of second-language learners while nurturing their dignity and self-respect. Lastly, we offer curricular guidelines to help teachers who are searching for ways to plan learning experiences that will benefit all students.

Self-Esteem and Literacy Development

Underlying our concept of an authentically active curriculum is a set of beliefs pertaining to language and literacy development that is applicable to teaching second-language learners. These beliefs are based on more than a decade of research on learners in real language-learning contexts, whether in the classroom, the home, or the community (Edelsky, Draper, & Smith, 1983; Heath, 1983; Ivener, 1990;

Slaughter, et al., 1985); they are informed by contemporary theory relevant to a whole language perspective (see, for example, Edelsky, Altwerger, & Flores, 1991; Goodman, 1986; Goodman, Smith, Meredith, & Goodman, 1987), as well as our considerable experience working with second-language learners and their teachers. Here we describe those beliefs that are particularly relevant to the issue of self-esteem in relation to literacy development.

1. *All students, including second-language learners, come to school with a great deal of experience with oral and written language communication.* Throughout their lives, students build and use literacy as they strive to understand and function successfully in their world. This has been documented by various ethnographic and qualitative studies of young children's awareness and use of environmental print and their involvement in meaningful and functional literacy events in the home and community (Cazden, 1981; Clay, 1982; Doake, 1985; Y.M. Goodman & Altwerger, 1981; Harste, Burke, & Woodward, 1982; Haussler, 1985; Heath, 1983; Taylor, 1983; Wilkinson, 1982). These studies suggest that it is not valid to assume that students, even those of low socioeconomic levels, minority cultures, or non-English-speaking backgrounds, lack basic knowledge of print and its uses, despite what reading readiness or other standardized reading tests may indicate. It is important for teachers to discern the literacy knowledge students have in both English and their primary language and to find ways to draw on and validate this knowledge in their classrooms.

2. *The language and literacy knowledge that language learners construct is influenced by the home and community culture and by varying degrees of contact with the larger society.* The communication competencies students bring to school reflect culturally based rules and expectations for language use in various situations. These rules and expectations for language use may differ from those of the teacher or school culture (Anderson & Stokes, 1984; Cook-Gumperz, 1986; Ferreiro & Teberosky, 1982; Heath, 1983). Students may enter the classroom with the

expectation that written language is always functional, meaningful, and predictable, only to find these expectations violated by decontextualized "reading" activities. There is a danger of underestimating the competence of these students based on their performance on inauthentic tasks. Teachers must appreciate that students will draw on all systems of language (graphophonic, syntactic, semantic, and pragmatic) to predict the meanings and purposes of literacy events in ways that are consistent with their cultural and societal backgrounds. Appreciation of knowledge students bring to school and critical examination of the authenticity of literacy events in the classroom are crucial in working with diverse student populations.

3. *Self-esteem and language are nurtured with encouragement and support from those who play a significant role in the student's life* (Altman & Chemers, 1980; Clark, 1984; Garcia, 1983; Halliday, 1975; Vygotsky, 1962). Cambourne (1988) asserts that language is learned most successfully when the learner is immersed in an environment in which other language users continually demonstrate the form and use of the language during meaningful communication rather than "model" that language for learners to imitate and repeat. Furthermore, language users should expect and accept approximations produced by language learners, thereby encouraging the risk-taking that is crucial to learning. This type of encouragement and support is most important for second-language learners in the classroom, because even after basic proficiency is achieved, the teacher and the students may not share all of the same knowledge about the linguistic and social systems that give meaning to language. Differences in what oral or written messages are intended to mean and what they are understood to mean are bound to arise. It is crucial to the self-esteem and language development of second-language learners that the teacher accept and support their interpretations and approximations of meaning and provide an environment rich in demonstrations of proficient language use.

4. *Language learners play active, collaborative roles in the social learning context.* It is widely accepted that both first- and second-language learners play active roles in their own language development. They participate fully in communicative contexts as they negotiate meaning with others. Whole language theory contends that learning is also facilitated when both teachers and students are active participants in the language-learning environment. For example, when topics and directions for inquiry are determined collaboratively, there is greater motivation for in-depth study by students, greater opportunity for students to apply relevant background knowledge, and greater motivation for them to use language and literacy as learning tools. Self-esteem is increased, because the value of each student's contribution is acknowledged and appreciated.

5. *Language develops through authentic language use, not language exercises.* Edelsky (1986) and Edelsky, Altwerger and Flores (1991) have drawn a distinction between language *exercises* and *authentic* language. Unlike language exercises, authentic language is used for real, meaningful purposes and is predictable and relevant to the language context. Children learning their first language are immersed in authentic language from birth as those around them carry out the various social tasks of everyday life. Likewise, young children use authentic language, if only in approximations of the adult form, as they attempt to communicate their needs and desires. The second-language learner requires the same environment both in and out of school. Meaningless worksheets and drills, too often the core of language programs, limit the second-language learner's access to authentic language and, in our view, inhibit learning. Success in language learning should rest not upon performance on contrived and artificial language exercises, but on the ability to communicate in natural language settings. Classrooms should provide students with many opportunities to interact with authentic, meaningful language across the curriculum.

Success: A Cultural Constraint for Second-Language Learners?

Most educators agree that self-esteem for second-language learners hinges on their actual or perceived academic success. There has been disagreement, however, about how success should be defined and evaluated, and whether it is even attainable for cultural and linguistic minorities in the present system of schooling. Educators used to assume that teaching students English would provide them with equal educational opportunity and prevent or remedy the school-failure and high drop-out rates that lead to poor integration into a nation's economic system. Paulston (1980) contends that programs based on this line of reasoning follow an "equilibrium" paradigm: teachers maintain society through achieving harmonious relationships in the classroom and expect a smooth, cumulative change by the second-language learner from minority to majority status. Over the years several explanations have been offered to account for the fact that this transition to majority status and consequent "success" does not occur for many language-minority students.

In the 1960s, a *deficit hypothesis* attempted to account for and remedy the "persistence of gross inequalities in the life opportunities of youth from different social classes and racial groups" (Deutsch, Katz, & Jensen, 1968, p. 1). This hypothesis held that "the language of students from different cultures is...inadequate for dealing with the complex uses of language required in educational contexts" (Flores, Cousin, & Díaz, 1991, p. 371). It followed from this view that the social component of education did not need a major overhaul: success was difficult for second-language learners to achieve because of an inherent deficiency in their first language and culture. In the 1970s and early 1980s, another explanation emerged as classroom research suggested that students collude with teachers and peers in organizing social structures to support their own subordination, low self-concept, and school failure (Kjolseth, 1972; McDermott & Gospodinoff, 1979; Wilcox, 1982). In this view, students act out the passivity, defiance, and ignorance that the system expects of them.

More recently, critical pedagogists have pointed out that "success" is strongly rooted in the values of the majority (Freire & Macedo, 1987; Giroux, 1983, 1988; McLaren, 1989). Schools have institutionalized different treatment of students on the basis of race, sex, culture, and class, through tracking, testing, and instructional practices. Rather than recommending that the problem of school failure be remedied by preparing students to succeed in terms defined by the majority culture, critical pedagogists call for a transformation of schools to reflect a more democratic and equitable system for defining and evaluating success. They urge educators to develop a pedagogy of resistance and hope (Giroux, 1983).

This last perspective, when combined with whole language theory, offers a powerful curriculum framework for supporting the development of both language and literacy and the self-esteem and personal dignity of all students.

A Curriculum for Building Self-Esteem

Family, friends, community, and school all play a role in a student's sense of self-esteem, but the power of the teacher, classroom, and curriculum together cannot be underestimated. In the context of the classroom, the teacher is the primary source of encouragement and support. Here the ESL student learns the power of language. Teachers who value students as individuals with unique capabilities are aware that language, be it spoken, written, or nonverbal, is a form of transaction that has the power to unite or separate people. Any classroom concerned with building self-esteem must first and foremost embrace the common and diverse strengths students bring to the classroom from their home cultures. Teachers must perceive all learners as capable of constructing and reconstructing meaning and knowledge over time. They need to provide opportunities for students to share their knowledge and questions and to view themselves as successful contributors to their own learning.

With this in mind, we present in what follows several key aspects of successful classrooms that are of particular relevance for second-language learners.

The Language and Literacy Environment

Teachers interested in meeting the needs of second-language learners while building on their communicative strengths are key partners and facilitators in the teaching and learning process. One powerful resource available to all teachers is the classroom itself. The physical attributes of the classroom, the materials it contains, and the activities it offers are valuable tools that support student learning. Research indicates that the classroom literacy environment extends the teacher's instructional strategies even when direct instruction is not going on (Loughlin & Ivener, 1988).

There is widespread agreement that inclusion of the home language of monolingual, bilingual, and multilingual students in the classroom is integral to their success. If students' home language is included in the curriculum and learning environment, they learn that this language is respected and valued. Monolingual teachers who are inhibited by their own language limits can include other languages in the classroom by reaching out to students and their families. Students can help prepare newsletters, posters, bulletin boards, awards, messages, and curriculum materials. For example, monolingual teachers in an Albuquerque elementary school recently enlisted the help of first- through fifth-graders to prepare multilingual invitations to a community curriculum-sharing night.

When teachers rely on the community to support learning experiences, they lessen the frustration often experienced in trying to obtain appropriate materials for use with ESL students. The neighborhood can be a rich resource for materials on such common themes as machines, transportation, housing, and so on. Students can participate in the collection of such material. Some teachers involve students in building classroom models of community stores, restaurants, and businesses (Edelsky, Altwerger, & Flores,

1991). This encourages conversation and the sharing of concrete knowledge, as well as critical thinking.

However, research indicates that the mere existence of a multilingual environment is not sufficient to engage students in actual literacy use (Ivener, 1990). Maintaining a functional and meaningful literacy environment is critical. For example, teachers in one whole language study group visited 16 classrooms and found that most of their print displays and bulletin boards, except for sign-up sheets, did not encourage student response (Ivener, 1983). Furthermore, student access to print varies greatly between instructional and transitional times of the day (Ivener, 1990). Teachers should observe their students' interaction with the literacy environment to determine whether full access is being achieved when desired.

All students are thinkers—knowledge seekers, problem solvers, and creators. A carefully planned, meaningful literacy environment that includes students' home language and culture creates a sense of community in which each student is valued and respected.

Social Contexts for Language Interaction

It has long been known that immersing and engaging language learners in multiple and varied communicative contexts is critical to language development. Traditionally, however, schools have been fairly sterile language environments that limit social contexts for authentic language use. Teachers do the majority of the talking in many classrooms, while students are confined to answering questions or participating in staged or artificial language exercises. When teachers devote time and effort to create social contexts within their classrooms, however, an increased involvement in students' functional and meaningful language use is noted. We view this social interaction as crucial for second-language learners.

While whole-group experiences provide the second-language learners with some opportunity to observe and interact with classmates, their willingness to communicate often increases in one-on-one and small-group settings. Traditional seating configurations, which isolate students and prevent collaboration and communication, must give way to arrangements that promote movement, peer interaction, and shared ownership of workspaces and materials. A committee structure that encourages students to work cooperatively on meaningful learning tasks is a good option.

Teachers can play a major role in promoting a positive social climate in the classroom. It is important to show a willingness to accept student responses, particularly those of second-language learners, in order to encourage ongoing, active participation in the classroom. This attitude of acceptance and inclusion is communicated to *all* students, encouraging a sense of community and cohesiveness involving ESL students and their English-speaking peers alike. Such community-building is illustrated by the way classmates responded to Marisela, who entered her first grade classroom with minimal English experience and limited literacy in her first language. The teacher had little knowledge of Marisela's native language but decided to partner her with children who enjoyed writing and were risk-takers in spelling. As part of their work and play the children made books about their activities and wrote a story about their times together. Together they read and reread their books. The other students coaxed Marisela to take the pencil and to use the books they made as references for their next book or story. At the same time, they asked Marisela for terms and labels in her native language. The children invented ways to communicate and showed mutual respect for differences.

Classroom teachers can make a difference in self-esteem, as is evident in classrooms in which a variety of social contexts are present. Teachers should involve second-language learners in many of the same social contexts that benefit monolingual learners: writing workshops, shared reading, literature studies, theme cycles, and authentic reasons to communicate with peers and adults in and out of the classroom. Acceptance of second-language learners' approximations of English in these activities is key to fostering a sense of accomplishment and self-esteem.

Theme cycles. Opportunities for students to develop a positive self-concept require their participation in the structure and content of classroom life. The *theme cycle* outlined in the figure is a framework that can be used to involve students in collaborative curriculum planning (Edelsky, Altwerger, & Flores, 1991). In contrast to traditional theme units that are planned by the teacher in order to present an integrated unit of study, theme cycles are planned and negotiated by both the students and the teacher in the classroom. Students are involved in choosing the topic for study (or issues within a topic), identifying a common store of knowledge on the topic, suggesting questions and issues for analysis and critique, planning the learning experiences, and representing and evaluating learning. Students *learn how to learn* as they participate in the critical problem-solving and language use inherent in the planning of theme studies.

Theme Cycle in Multilingual Classrooms

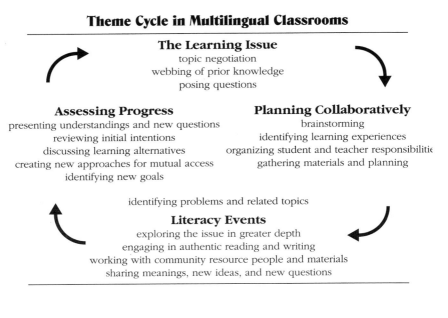

The Learning Issue
topic negotiation
webbing of prior knowledge
posing questions

Assessing Progress
presenting understandings and new questions
reviewing initial intentions
discussing learning alternatives
creating new approaches for mutual access
identifying new goals

Planning Collaboratively
brainstorming
identifying learning experiences
organizing student and teacher responsibilitie
gathering materials and planning

identifying problems and related topics
Literacy Events
exploring the issue in greater depth
engaging in authentic reading and writing
working with community resource people and materials
sharing meanings, new ideas, and new questions

Altwerger & Ivener

The theme cycle allows second-language learners to contribute, even if contributions are communicated in students' first languages. It reveals the knowledge that second-language students have and often enlightens the teacher about their home cultures. It immerses students in authentic language and literacy use as they read, write, speak, and listen in order to answer their own questions. Most important, it develops in all students a sense that their knowledge and questions are appreciated and their participation, however limited it might be, is valued.

Although students are involved in developing topics of study in the theme cycle, teachers should ensure that those selected are worthwhile. Some topics may offer limited opportunities for ESL students to learn about issues significant to their lives or to engage in critical investigation or debate. For example, themes such as chocolate, pandas, or jewelry offer limited opportunities for students to examine the realities of everyday life, and they do not prepare students to solve problems in their own lives, their communities, or society as a whole. Topics such as change, nature, technology, ecology, and poverty offer more potential for critical analysis, provided that the prior knowledge of the ESL and English-speaking students is solicited and respected.

Authentic Assessment

Assessing success should be a collaborative endeavor between teacher and student that relates to the student's ability to use and incorporate what is gained from various learning experiences (see chapter 9 of this volume). Learning experiences themselves provide the means of ongoing assessment. Both the teacher and the student should participate in researching, planning, and gathering materials for evaluation and in monitoring progress. Recently, many educators (Goodman, Goodman, & Hood, 1989; Tierney, Carter, & Desai, 1991) have described the merits of portfolio assessment as a means of tracking student progress in language and literacy throughout the school year. Most stress the need for student involvement in choosing samples of work for assessment and for student participation with the teacher in evaluating progress toward mutually determined goals.

It is important to track second-language learners' progress in use of English. Standardized language assessments provide little information in regard to students' actual abilities to use language meaningfully for a variety of purposes. Teachers and students should collect language samples—such as journal entries, written reports and projects, published pieces, and letters—that demonstrate the students' range of writing. Similarly, records of students' reading may include books and novels read but should also include functional reading, such as use of phone books, informational materials, recipes, and directions. In addition, oral language development should be tracked through the use of observational records and careful "kid-watching" (Y.M. Goodman, 1985). Attention to students' developing ability and willingness to communicate with others should balance a focus on the form of the language used.

Authentic assessment of student progress provides teachers with valuable information with which to plan curricula that best meet the needs of their students. It also helps students appreciate their own achievements and view themselves as competent, capable learners.

Classroom Principles

The development of language and self-esteem for second-language learners occurs when classrooms are planned on the basis of sound principles of language learning and high democratic ideals. Students must know that their home language and culture are viewed as assets rather than obstacles to learning. They must be afforded full access to meaningful language and literacy experiences and participation in the sort of critical problem solving that leads to both individual and social well-being.

References
Altman, I., & Chemers, M. (1980). Cultural aspects of environment-behavior relationships. In H. Triandis & R. Brislin

(Eds.), *Handbook of crosscultural psychology: Social psychology*. Boston, MA: Allyn & Bacon.

Anderson, A., & Stokes, S. (1984). Social and institutional influences on the development and practice of literacy. In H. Goelman, A. Oberg, & F. Smith (Eds.), *Awakening to literacy*. London: Heinemann.

Apple, M. (1982). *Ideology and education*. Boston, MA: Routledge & Kegan Paul.

Cambourne, B. (1988). *The whole story*. Auckland, New Zealand: Scholastic.

Cazden, C. (1981). Language development and the preschool environment. In C. Cazden (Ed.), *Language in early childhood education*. Washington, DC: National Association for the Education of Young Children.

Clark, M.M. (1984). Literacy at home and at school: Insights from a study of young fluent readers. In H. Goelman, A. Oberg, & F. Smith (Eds.), *Awakening to literacy*. London: Heinemann.

Clay, M. (1982) *Observing young children: Selected papers*. Portsmouth, NH: Heinemann.

Collier, V.P. (1987). Age and rate of acquisition of second language for academic purposes. *TESOL Quarterly, 21,* 617–641.

Cook-Gumperz, J. (1986). Literacy and schooling: An unchanging equation? In J. Cook-Gumperz (Ed.), *The social construction of literacy*. New York: Cambridge University Press.

Cummins, J. (1981). Age on arrival and immigrant second language learning in Canada: A reassessment. *Applied Linguistics, 2,* 132–149.

Deutsch, M., Katz, I., & Jensen, A.R. (1968). *Social class, race and psychological development*. New York: Holt, Rinehart.

Doake, D. B. (1985). Reading-like behavior: Its role in learning to read. In A. Jaggar & M.T. Smith-Burke (Eds.), *Observing the language learner*. Newark, DE: International Reading Association.

Edelsky, C. (1986). *Writing in a bilingual program: Habia una vez*. Norwood, NJ: Ablex.

Edelsky, C., Altwerger, B., & Flores, B. (1991). *Whole language: What's the difference?* Portsmouth, NH: Heinemann.

Edelsky, C., Draper, K., & Smith, K. (1983). Hookin' 'em in at the start of school in a "whole language" classroom. *Anthropology & Education Quarterly, 14,* 257–281.

Ferreiro, E., & Teberosky, A. (1982). *Literacy before schooling*. Portsmouth, NH: Heinemann.

Flores, B., Cousin, P.T, & Díaz, E. (1991). Transforming deficit myths about learning, language, and culture. *Language Arts, 68,* 369–379.

Freire, P., & Macedo, D. (1987). *Literacy: Reading the word and reading the world.* South Hadley, MA: Bergin & Garvey.

Garcia, E. (1983). *Early childhood bilingualism with special reference to the Mexican-American child.* Albuquerque, NM: University of New Mexico.

Giroux, H. (1983). *Theory and resistance in education: A pedagogy for the opposition.* London: Heinemann.

Giroux, H. (1988). *Teachers as intellectuals.* South Hadley, MA: Bergin & Garvey.

Goodman, K. (1986). *What's whole in whole language?* Portsmouth, NH: Heinemann.

Goodman, K., Goodman, Y., & Hood, W. (1989). *The whole language evaluation book.* Portsmouth, NH: Heinemann.

Goodman, K., Smith, E., Meredith, R., & Goodman, Y.M. (1987). *Language and thinking in school: A whole language curriculum* (3rd ed.). New York: Richard C. Owen.

Goodman, Y.M. (1985). Kidwatching: Observing children in the classroom. In A. Jaggar & M.T. Smith-Burke (Eds.), *Observing the language learner.* Newark, DE, and Urbana, IL: International Reading Association and the National Council of Teachers of English.

Goodman, Y.M., & Altwerger, B. (1981, September). *Print awareness in preschool children,* (Occasional Paper No. 4). Tucson, AZ: College of Education, University of Arizona.

Halliday, M.A.K. (1975). *Learning how to mean: Explorations in the development of language.* London: Edward Arnold.

Harste, J., Burke, C., & Woodward, V. (1982). Children's language and world: Initial encounters with print. In J.A. Langer & M.T. Smith-Burke (Eds.), *Reader meets author/bridging the gap.* Newark, DE: International Reading Association.

Haussler, M.M. (1985). A young child's developing concepts of print. In A. Jaggar & M.T. Smith-Burke (Eds.), *Observing the language learner.* Newark, DE: International Reading Association.

Heath, S.B. (1983). *Ways with words.* Cambridge, UK: Cambridge University Press.

Ivener, B.L. (1983). Inservice: A teacher-chosen direction for creating environments for literacy. *The New Mexico Journal of Reading, 3* (2), 712.

Ivener, B.L. (1990, Summer). *Primary grade children's use of the environment and the social context of their spontaneous writing.* Unpublished doctoral dissertation, University of New Mexico, Albuquerque.

Kjolseth, R. (1972). Bilingual education programs in the United States: For assimilation or pluralism? In B. Spolsky (Ed.), *The*

language education of minority children: Selected readings.
Rowley, MA: Newbury House.

Loughlin, C., & Ivener, B.L. (1988, April). *Literacy behaviors of kindergarten and primary children in high stimulus-level literacy environments.* Paper presented at the Research Symposium of the Association for Childhood Education International, Salt Lake City, UT.

McDermott, R.P. (1987). Achieving school failure. In H. Singer & R.B. Ruddell (Eds), *Theoretical models and processes of reading* (3rd ed.). Newark, DE: International Reading Association.

McDermott, R.P., & Gospodinoff, K. (1979). Social contexts for ethnic borders and school failure. In A. Wolfgang (Ed.), *Nonverbal behavior: Applications and cultural implications.* New York: Academic.

McLaren, P. (1989). *Life in schools: An introduction to critical pedagogy in the foundations of education.* White Plains, NY: Longman.

Paulston, C.B. (1980). *Bilingual education: Theories and issues.* Rowley, MA: Newbury House.

Slaughter, H., Haussler, M., Franks, A., Jilbert, K., Chapter 1 and the Department of Legal and Research Services of Tucson, & Silentman, I. (1985, April). *Contextual differences in oral and written discourse during early literacy instruction.* Paper presented at the annual meeting of the American Educational Research Association, Chicago, IL.

Taylor, D. (1983). *Family literacy.* Portsmouth, NH: Heinemann.

Tierney, R., Carter, M., & Desai, L. (1991). *Portfolio assessment in the reading-writing classroom.* Norwood, NJ: Christopher-Gordon.

Vygotsky, L.S. (1962). *Thought and language.* Cambridge, MA: MIT Press.

Wilcox, K. (1982). Differential socialization in the classroom: Implications for equal opportunity. In G. Spindler (Ed.), *Doing the ethnography of schooling: Educational anthropology in action.* New York: Holt, Rinehart.

Wilkinson, L.C. (Ed.). (1982). *Communicating in the classroom.* New York: Academic.

Anna Uhl Chamot
J. Michael O'Malley

5

Instructional Approaches and Teaching Procedures

Students learning English as a new language face many challenges and frustrations as they seek to make sense of the school environment. Perhaps the most critical task they encounter is learning how to read a language in which they have limited proficiency. Native-English speakers learning to read encounter words and grammatical structures that they can already understand orally. The second-language learner, whether learning to read for the first time or trying to transfer reading skills learned in the native language, encounters an inordinate amount of unfamiliar language even in beginning texts. Beginning readers who are native-English speakers expect to understand the text once they have managed to decode it; for the reader who is learning English, the text may not be comprehended even if it can be decoded.

In the first section of this chapter we identify the goals that are typical of ESL programs and describe how these relate to classroom objectives. In the second section we examine a number of instructional approaches for teaching English as a second language, identifying those that have a clearly stated approach for reading instruction. Then we suggest guidelines for the classroom teacher to use in assisting English learners to comprehend what they read. We conclude by identifying specific differences between reading instruction for native-English speakers and for students learning English.

First, however, we would like to clarify the terminology we use. English as a second language, or ESL, programs refer to approaches designed to teach English to speakers of other languages. An ESL program may be a component of a bilingual program in which students' native language is also used for instruction, or it may be a stand-alone program. Although for many non-native speakers, English may not be the second language learned but the third or fourth, we will refer to these students as ESL students for the sake of convenience. The term limited-English-proficient or LEP is widely used to describe ESL students, but we (and others) find it to be a negative and even pejorative term because of its emphasis on what students are unable to do rather than on what they are learning to do. Finally, we have decided not to use the terms "mainstream" or "regular" to describe classrooms in which the school's curriculum is delivered through the medium of English that has not been modified for non-native speakers. To use these terms implies that students in ESL or bilingual classes are somehow outside the school's main program and are "irregular" in some way. Instead, we will adopt the term suggested by Enright and McCloskey (1988) and refer to classrooms designed for native-English-speaking students as *grade-level* classrooms.

Goals of ESL Programs

The major goal of ESL programs is to provide students with the language skills they need to be successful in grade-level classrooms and to accomplish this in as short a period as possible. The goal seems obvious, but both the goal and the means of attaining it are exceedingly complex and have changed considerably in recent years. Communicative skills, or the ability to interact socially in English, used to be considered a sufficient criterion for assigning students to grade-level classrooms. Now we recognize that, to be successful in school, students need more than social-language skills; they need academic-language skills, which involve using both receptive and productive language for thinking and reasoning in all content areas.

The level and type of academic language needed for success in grade-level classrooms has not been adequately defined or researched. We know that academic language includes an emphasis on reading and writing, but the types of oral skills required in grade-level classrooms are not easily determined. Cummins (1980) indicates that cognitive academic language is characterized as context-reduced language used for cognitively demanding tasks (see chapter 3 of this volume). Context-reduced language lacks accompanying cues that assist comprehension, such as facial expression, body language, visuals, or experiential activities. Cognitively demanding tasks require learners to manipulate concepts, solve problems, and learn new and often challenging information. These tasks require specialized language and language structures that vary depending on the content area. In grade-level classrooms, cognitively demanding tasks are frequently presented to students through context-reduced language, particularly at upper elementary and secondary levels. We suggest further that a complete definition of academic language proficiency should include abilities in academic language functions such as explaining, describing, and classifying, along with higher order thinking skills such as analyzing, synthesizing, and evaluating (Chamot & O'Malley, 1994; O'Malley, 1991).

While the development of academic-language competence represents the major goal of many ESL programs, other goals are also important. Community survival skills, social communicative competence, subject matter knowledge, and reading across the curriculum are additional goals that an ESL program might espouse.

ESL Instructional Approaches

In the past, language-teaching approaches in the United States were developed to teach a foreign language to native speakers of English rather than to teach English as a second language to speakers of other languages. This foreign-language emphasis has shaped methodologies according to instructional goals that changed over the years. Prior to World War I, for example, the accepted approach was the Direct Method, which sought to develop oral skills through a series of questions and answers between teacher and student, conducted exclusively in the foreign language (Richards & Rodgers, 1986). This contrasts with the Grammar Translation Method, popular in the first half of this century, which focused on the development of reading skills in the foreign language through translation and extensive grammatical explanations in the students' native language (Ovando & Collier, 1985). A return to an oral skills emphasis characterizes language-teaching approaches that have developed in the second half of the 20th century. Almost all these started as foreign-language approaches for secondary or adult students and have been applied with little modification to the teaching of English as a second language to school-aged students. While most approaches continue to focus on oral skills, instruction in reading and writing has been added in recent years to most ESL programs. In the following we discuss some major types of instructional approaches used in ESL classrooms and provide brief descriptions of typical activities associated with each approach.

The Audiolingual Method

While this was *the* language-teaching method of the 1950s and 1960s, it subsequently was criticized on both linguistic and psychological grounds, and today's ESL educators generally eschew its practice. However, its techniques and procedures continue to be used in classrooms and to appear as drills in a number of ESL textbooks (Chamot & Stewner-Manzanares, 1985; Richards & Rodgers, 1986). This method is based on a behavioral view of learning that sees language as a set of habits to be acquired through rote repetition, memorization without attention to meaning, and manipulation of sentence elements. While students in sur-vival-level ESL classes might conceivably benefit from mem-orizing certain useful formulas through audiolingual meth-ods, the approach does not lend itself to social communica-tion. Since the audiolingual method focuses on the devel-opment of oral-language skills, reading and writing are introduced only after students have had extensive practice with oral drills. In practice, this leads to a neglect of literacy development in the new language.

Communicative Approaches

Approaches that emphasize the development of interpersonal communicative skills as the major goal in lan-guage learning include Communicative Language Teaching (CLT) and the Natural Approach. In these approaches stu-dents take part in a variety of oral language activities in which they use the new language for meaningful communi-cation rather than for rote repetition (Krashen & Terrell, 1983; Nattinger, 1984; Savignon, 1983). These approaches are generally based on theories of communicative compe-tence (Canale & Swain, 1980) and on the Monitor Model, which claims that communicative competence is acquired unconsciously (Krashen, 1982). Communicative approaches have been criticized for promoting fluency in the language at the expense of accuracy (Hammerly, 1991), and ques-tions have also been raised about their suitability for for-eign- and second-language teaching (Richards & Rodgers, 1986) and their appropriateness for developing academic-language skills (Chamot & O'Malley, 1994).

Communicative Language Teaching. Communicative Language Teaching, like other communicative approaches, focuses on developing communicative proficiency rather than mastering grammatical structures (Chamot & Stewner-Manzanares, 1985; Richards & Rodgers, 1986). The CLT cur-riculum is organized around the language functions needed for interactive communication (for example, greeting, request-ing, apologizing) and semantic topics or notions (time, loca-tion, frequency, and so on), rather than around a strict grammatical sequence (Wilkins, 1976). CLT activities include role playing, simulation games, small-group work, and information-gap activities in which students must exchange information in order to complete a task (Richards & Rodgers; Savignon, 1983). While the focus of CLT is on the development of oral proficiency, reading and writing activities may also be incorporated into instruction. Authentic reading materials such as advertisements, menus, newspaper articles, and signs are preferred to linguistically modified texts even for beginning level students (Richards & Rodgers; Wilkins).

The Natural Approach. This approach, described by Krashen and Terrell (1983), and Terrell (1981) is probably the best known communicative approach for school-aged ESL students in U.S. schools. The main goal of this approach is to develop students' ability to engage in basic oral and written communication (Krashen & Terrell). All students are believed to progress through the same stages in language acquisition; the first stage is a silent one in which students amass language through listening to comprehensible input from English speakers. Teachers using this approach provide input in natural English at a level just slightly beyond the learners' current level of proficiency and do not encourage students to speak before they are ready. When speech emerges, students typically use one- or two-word utterances to respond to questions and communicate their ideas. Errors are not corrected, for it is assumed that students will gradually correct their own errors as they receive more input. Reading and writing are taught as natural extensions of listening and speaking, and many and varied opportunities are provided for students to experience literacy. Students in ESL classrooms where the Natural Approach is used may be quite proficient in their ability to interact socially with English speakers, but their academic-language skills may be less developed.

Approaches to Reading Instruction

Approaches for teaching reading to native-English-speaking children have frequently been used with ESL students with little modification. This is surprising, given the differences between first- and second-language reading. In some cases, reading instruction that is for primary grade children is used with ESL students at upper elementary or secondary levels. The native-language beginning reader is proficient in oral language and rarely encounters words or grammatical structures in reading that are not already known orally. The second-language reader, on the other hand, constantly faces the task of trying to understand a text containing words and structures that even if decoded successfully are still not comprehended because they are not within the reader's oral language knowledge. Finally, the ESL beginning reader may or may not be literate in the first language. If the student is already literate, it is often assumed that reading skills will transfer to English reading (Cummins, 1980; Krashen & Biber, 1988), although there is some evidence that such transfer may not take place automatically (Clark, 1979; McLaughlin, 1987).

Many educators believe that first language literacy should be achieved prior to introducing the ESL student to reading in English (Ovando & Collier, 1985). While this seems logical, it does present some concerns. For example, if the transfer of literacy from the first language to English is not automatic, then teachers may need to show students the strategies needed to transfer their prior knowledge and reading skills to the new language. A practical concern in teaching native-language reading is the scarcity of reading materials and multilingual teachers. A second practical concern is time: an ESL student arriving in the United States at age 13 or 14 may not have enough years of schooling left in which to learn to read in both the native language and English, desirable as the goal of biliteracy may be. In our view, the ESL reading approaches discussed so far have not adequately addressed these issues.

Code-based or phonics instruction. The debate over bottom-up reading instruction (such as phonics) and top-down instruction (such as the whole language approach) is as heated in the ESL and bilingual fields as it is in the broader education community. Proponents of phonics for ESL students assert that a thorough grounding in sound-symbol correspondences and extensive drill in sounding out English words is necessary for developing reading ability in non-native-English speakers. A problem with this approach is that even if a student can sound out a word more or less accurately, the word may not be recognized because it is not a part of the student's oral vocabulary. A second problem is that ESL students who are trying to sound out a word in English may base their pronunciation on the same or similar phonemes in the native language. This is generally corrected by the teacher but may persist as students rely on their prior knowledge about sound-symbol correspondences. When this happens, the reading lesson becomes a pronunciation lesson and comprehension may be neglected.

Language experience approach. In this approach, students dictate their own experiences or stories to a teacher or scribe. This text is then used as a reading text for its author and perhaps also for other students in the class. The advantage of the language experience approach for ESL students is the same as for native-English speakers: students are not asked to read anything that is unfamiliar or outside their own experience and language knowledge. Rigg (1989) reports success with this approach to beginning reading instruction for ESL students of varying ages, including adults. However, the language experience approach is not intended to be the sole approach to reading, for students also need to learn how to read texts written by others.

Whole language approaches. Whole language is more a philosophy than a method. It is based on the belief that language should not be fragmented into its component parts, but should be learned and used as a whole system of communication. This means that listening, reading, speaking, and writing are integrated into the reading and language arts curriculum, rather than being separated into skill areas such as phonics, decoding, reading for comprehension, handwriting, spelling, guided writing, and composition. Students are provided with many opportunities to interact with text and to use language for their own purposes. Principles of the language experience approach are frequently incorporated into whole language instruction, and to these types of literacy experiences are added discussion and writing activities that focus on the uses of language in students' life experiences. Children's literature and other authentic texts (rather than basal readers) are used in whole language classrooms. Typical class activities include reading aloud by the teacher, journal writing, writing stories based on the pattern of a previously read story, sustained silent reading, and conferences with the teacher or other students about reading and writing tasks.

Whole language approaches are rich in suggestions on *what* should be read and experienced but are less specific on *how* reading should be taught or performed by the student. This contrasts with current research that examines reading strategies and instructional approaches that develop text comprehension and higher order thinking skills (Brown, Armbruster, & Baker, 1986; Garner, 1987; Paris & Winograd, 1990). We do not believe that the what of reading needs to be in opposition to the how of reading. Any type of text—whether literary, utilitarian, or specially written for beginning readers—can be understood more completely when readers apply strategies that help them use their prior knowledge, read selectively, monitor their comprehension, summarize the text, and evaluate their own level of comprehension (Brown et al., 1983; Brown & Palincsar, 1982; Derry, 1990; Palincsar & Brown, 1986; Paris & Winograd, 1990). Our suggestions for instruction in reading strategies are summarized in the next section, under the approach that we have designed for developing the academic-language proficiency of ESL students (Chamot & O'Malley, 1987, 1994; O'Malley, 1988; O'Malley & Chamot, 1990).

Content-Based ESL Approaches

In recent years the differences between social communicative language and academic-language proficiency have been analyzed by a number of second-language researchers (Chamot & O'Malley, 1987, 1992; Collier, 1987, 1989; Cummins, 1984; O'Malley, 1991; O'Malley & Chamot, 1990). This analysis has allowed researchers to begin to identify the academic-language skills required for successful participation in grade-level classrooms and to propose integrated approaches to teaching language and other curricular content. Academic-language skills do not exist in a vacuum, for they entail the use of language to understand and react to school subjects such as science, mathematics, social studies, and literature. Integration of language and content for ESL learners can take a variety of forms. For example, content topics can be introduced into the language classroom, language-sensitive or "sheltered" instruction can be provided in the content classroom, or an integrated language and content curriculum can be designed (Chamot & Stewner-Manzanares, 1985; Crandall, 1987; Krashen, 1985; Mohan, 1986; Snow, Met, & Genesee, 1989; Spanos, 1990).

Sheltered instruction. In this approach, content teachers provide instruction to ESL students through a modified curriculum. Two specific modifications are for teachers to provide additional context to students through visual aids and to adjust their language so that it becomes comprehensible for students (Krashen, 1985). While these content teachers may be sensitive to students' language learning needs, they usually do not provide special instruction for developing language skills (Brinton, Snow, & Wesche, 1989; Freeman, Freeman, & Gonzalez, 1987; National Clearinghouse for Bilingual Education, 1987; Northcutt & Watson, 1986). Many sheltered programs are based on principles of learning that hold that students can acquire a new language through unconscious processes that are activated by comprehensible input in an anxiety-free setting.

The Cognitive Academic Language Learning Approach (CALLA). This content-based approach contrasts with sheltered instruction in that it derives from a cognitive model of learning and its learning-strategy instruction is integrated into content and language activities. CALLA is based on the belief that second language learners, like all learners, are mentally active and consciously aware of their own learning processes (Chamot & O'Malley, 1986, 1987, 1989, 1992; O'Malley, 1988, 1991; O'Malley & Chamot, 1990). CALLA instruction uses high-priority content drawn from the grade-level curriculum and identified by or in conjunction with content teachers. Added to the content are language activities designed to develop the vocabulary, oral skills, and reading and writing skills that will allow students to think and reason about the conceptual knowledge presented. The third component of CALLA is explicit instruction in learning strategies that are viewed as essential aids to the comprehension, storage, and recall of information and skills related to both content and language. Learning strategies are purposeful behaviors or thoughts that the learner uses to acquire and retain new information or skills (Pressley, 1988; Weinstein & Mayer, 1986). Learning strategies may be observable, as in the case of study skills such as note-taking or outlining, or nonobservable, as in monitoring comprehension, activating prior knowledge, or making inferences. A challenge for learning-strategy instruction is to make the "invisible" strategies visible to students through activities and materials that explain and foster their use.

CALLA's method of reading instruction is based on cognitive theory, which holds that reading comprehension involves interaction between the reader's purpose, prior knowledge, and text characteristics. This interactive process operates most effectively when readers make use of strategies that assist their comprehension. Skilled readers use a variety of strategic approaches to extract meaning from text, whereas less skilled readers use different strategies or use the strategies less effectively (Pressley, 1988). A substantial body of research in English-language contexts indicates that strategies that increase reading comprehension can be taught successfully to poor readers and that increased strategy use is maintained over time (Jones et al., 1987; Palincsar & Brown, 1986). One of the important components of successful strategy instruction is metacognitive awareness or understanding of what the task demands, recognizing similarities with tasks previously experienced, and recognizing and successfully deploying strategies needed to perform the task (Brown et al., 1983).

Some of the reading strategies taught in CALLA that expand the students' strategic repertoire are as follows:

1. *Elaboration, or active use of prior knowledge.* This could involve an activity in which students work individually or cooperatively to list or illustrate their knowledge about a topic before reading.

2. *Planning, or setting a purpose for reading.* Students decide why they will read a story or informational text. Reasons might be enjoyment, appreciation, understanding of an issue or viewpoint, or information. Planning helps readers make decisions about how they will approach the text. Will they read from beginning to end? Should they look at the headings and questions first to guide their reading? Should they skim quickly or read slowly?

3. *Monitoring comprehension by asking oneself questions such as: "Am I understanding this? Does it make sense?"* When readers become aware of comprehension breakdowns they can take action to remedy them. For example, they can use a strategy such as inferencing or questioning for clarification.

4. *Self-evaluation or assessing how well one has achieved the purpose set for reading.* Self-evaluation can take a number of forms, including discussion in cooperative groups, oral or written summaries or retelling, self-ratings, and learning logs.

As with other procedures, reading skills need to be practiced within the reading experience, rather than as separate components or independent skills. What this means is that readers need to experience text in its entirety first and then work on any component skills that are actually needed for full comprehension. Ways in which readers can experience an entire text before they are able to read and comprehend each word include first reading familiar words for the gist or main topic only, listening to the text, or participating in an activity such as reciprocal teaching (Palincsar & Brown, 1984, 1986) in which students work in cooperative groups to help one another comprehend a text.

In CALLA, reading skills are developed concurrently with other academic language skills. Students discuss what they read, listen to the teacher and other students reading, write stories to be read by themselves and others, and write about their own reading processes and experiences. CALLA emphasizes reading across the curriculum, not only in language arts. In this way it provides many opportunities for students to encounter authentic texts of differing types. Students develop academic language skills through listening, reading, talking, and writing about content from all areas of the curriculum. For example, in addition to reading stories, poems, and biographies, they might read for information in a science or social studies book or practice comprehension skills with mathematics word problems. Students are taught learning strategies in order to integrate top-down with bottom-up approaches to reading. Teachers encourage students to evaluate their own progress in reading and to verbalize and discuss their reading strategies with other students. However, teachers also monitor student progress in CALLA using alternative assessment procedures based on systematic observation and ratings of integrated language tasks.

In sum, CALLA's method of reading instruction for second language learners is to provide students with authentic texts that include both content area material and literature, to integrate oral- and written-language skills so that students can develop all aspects of academic language, and to develop strategic reading and writing through explicit instruction in learning strategies.

What the Classroom Teacher Can Do

Teachers of students learning English as a second language will probably encounter a diverse group even when their students are all from the same language background. As noted above, the students may differ in important instructional characteristics such as age, degree of literacy in the native language, background experiences and knowledge, and level of educational attainment. All of these characteristics will influence their responsiveness to reading instruction and, perhaps more basically, their understanding of the importance and uses of print. When students are from various language backgrounds, with different levels of orthographic and phonemic similarity to English, teachers will encounter a range of levels of difficulty in learning to read among students.

Because of this extraordinary diversity, it is problematic to identify a set of activities that can be expected to work for all students. Despite this, however, we believe that there are some *basic* instructional activities that effectively support the efforts of *most* students learning to read English. These are outlined here, with the understanding that certain instructional activities in the repertoire can be combined or modified to adapt to the needs of individual students. We do not adopt a particular theoretical view of reading in these recommendations; nor have we elected to give the approach we describe a name, since different combinations of activities are suitable for some students but not for others. However, those who have experience in programs such as Reading Recovery and reciprocal teaching will find some familiar elements here, as will those who advocate introducing literacy in an integrative manner with other language skills and a language experience approach. Perhaps more than any other view, however, we are influenced by cognitive theory as expressed in our previous work (O'Malley & Chamot, 1990; O'Malley, Chamot, & Walker, 1987) and by others (see, for example, Carrell, Devine, & Eskey, 1988).

Collect information on the students' literacy skills in their first language. Begin by finding out as much as possible about the students' level of literacy in their native language and their experience with literacy tasks. While direct administration of a standardized reading test may be possible in only a few languages other than English, teachers can nevertheless obtain information from students or from parents about students' educational background and literacy, relying on an aide or community liaison for translations if needed. For students who are literate in their first language, teachers will be able to draw parallels between the first language and English by teaching the students to use cognates that may exist between the two languages while inferring the meaning of unfamiliar words, and to use the strategies that were most effective for them in comprehending and retaining information from print material in their native language. For students who are not literate, depending on the students' age, the teacher may need to work on the meaning of print materials, their use in school and in daily life, and the fact that letters and sounds combine to make words and meaningful messages in written communication.

Activate the students' prior knowledge and cultural context. For any reading passage, determine what students know about the topic prior to the reading assignment. Students may need a reminder to activate this information from memory because they assume that anything learned in their native language has no bearing on information presented in English. By accessing information in long-term memory, students can predict the structure and content of information presented in the text, infer the meaning of unfamiliar words, check the new information against what is already known, and augment or modify that prior knowledge. If students have little familiarity with the topic of a reading passage, effort should be expended to develop students' knowledge about the topic through peer discussions, pictures, diagrams, drawings, filmstrips, videos, role-playing, and so on. One useful approach is for cooperative learning groups that are heterogeneous in English proficiency to discuss and share information on topics to be presented in upcoming reading passages. Depending on their level of proficiency in English, students may need to rely initially on their native language in discussions with other students.

Read daily to students. ESL students of all ages and levels of reading proficiency benefit from listening to stories, poems, and informational texts. This is especially beneficial to students unacquainted with literacy in their native language, because it provides them with opportunities to experience a piece of literature or gain information from expository text even before they have developed the ability to read such texts independently. Select materials which are age-appropriate and contain pictures or illustrations. Read high-interest materials that students have adequate vocabulary to understand but that may also challenge them. At the outset select materials that have a recurring organizational pattern such as a collection of folktales so you can discuss the structure of the text and ask students to predict what comes next. If the class also contains students who are literate in English, have these students read to the students with fewer literacy skills. Embed instruction on letter recognition and phonological awareness in the context of this meaningful reading rather than teaching these as discrete skills. Follow the reading with discussions of the meaning of the text, possible alternative interpretations, and predictions of what will come next. This will convey to students the meaning and uses of print.

Model and teach learning strategies explicitly. Students can use a variety of learning strategies to improve their comprehension of text and their retention of important information. These include such top-down strategies as scanning to obtain an overview of the text structure and major ideas, asking themselves questions about what they want to know from the text, predicting answers or information in forthcoming paragraphs, looking for specific words or concepts, inferring the meaning of unfamiliar words, taking notes, and summarizing important information. Students who already use some of these strategies for reading in their native language may need reminders that they can be used in English as well. Even students with beginning-level skills in English can scan for familiar words that can give cues to the topic and structure of a reading passage. Students who are not familiar with strategies for reading will profit from having them modeled by other students or by the teacher. Strategies should be taught by naming the strategy, indicating that the purpose of the strategy is to help the student comprehend and remember new information, and reminding the student to use strategies with subsequent reading passages. Teachers should encourage students to participate in peer discussions about their most useful strategies, which enables them to verbalize strategies, hear other students discuss strategies, and gradually build a repertoire of strategic approaches to reading.

Have students read for different purposes. Students need exposure to different types of materials of varying difficulty and on different topics. Beginning readers should be given high-interest reading selections containing familiar vocabulary so that they can build up their reading speed and accuracy. The terms *real* and *authentic* are often used to describe literature that represents quality writing and that should have high interest for students. What is interesting to students will differ depending on their age and the type of program in which they are enrolled. Also select materials in English from the students' own cultural backgrounds, and ask students to bring in reading materials from home. Most students enjoy age-appropriate literature, but some students may also want direct exposure to authentic grade-level materials in content areas or, for older students, to occupationally relevant materials. Point out the different purposes of written texts to give students a broad understanding of print materials.

Emphasize comprehension over pronunciation. Engage students in teacher-directed or cooperative group discussions that emphasize comprehension. Cooperative groups should be heterogeneous in English proficiency to capitalize on different levels of reading and comprehension. Model the asking of higher order thinking skills questions and encourage students to ask these questions in their discussions. With literature, describe the major elements of a story's plot, characters, themes, and importance; in content areas, focus on text structure and main ideas. If students read aloud, avoid correcting pronunciation because, inevitably, excessive time will be invested in correcting rather than in reading. Take notes on mispronunciations and miscues when students read aloud in order to understand the types of difficulties students are experiencing and to review students' progress over time. These notes can be used to identify phonemes, individual words, and intonation patterns that should be pointed out and modeled in the context of meaningful stories that are read to the students. It should be remembered, however, that reading comprehension depends on finding meaning in a text, not on being able to pronounce every word correctly.

Teach writing at the same time as reading. For beginning-level students, start with a language experience approach in which the teacher or an aide transcribes a story that students dictate after they have developed it individually or collectively. These stories can be handwritten in large print on a chalkboard or paper and should be copied over by students so that they have their own record of the stories they have created and can read them later. Student stories should be written exactly as they are dictated. The teacher should use correct spelling but preserve students' sentence structures, even if they are incomplete or ungrammatical (Rigg, 1989). Only in this way can students feel ownership of their stories. When students gain more proficiency in English, they will begin to edit and revise their stories to conform to the models that they are listening to and reading. Students should begin writing their own stories as soon as possible and can be asked to bring stories, fables, and experiences from their own culture to school. Writing should be done in different media (paper and pencil, chalkboard, computer, and so on) and for different purposes (to share experiences with a friend, tell a story, explain a concept, show a sequence of activities, persuade another person, or summarize information). Use a process approach to writing in which students plan, write, edit, revise, and discuss their writing with others.

Assess students' progress in reading and involve students in self-evaluation. Use multiple measures of reading progress that reflect comprehension and interest, not just skills. Such measures might include checklists of oral reading performance, reading strategies the student uses, reading comprehension skills ("comprehends oral stories," "literal comprehension," "inferential comprehension," and so on), interests ("reads for pleasure," "selects books independently," "samples a variety of materials"), and applications ("participates in reading groups," "writes dialogue journal entries"). Encourage students to maintain a dialogue journal with you in which they assess their own progress as readers. Include all observations, checklists, and the students' self-assessments in individual portfolios that are used to maintain information on students, to communicate with other teachers about the students' progress, to communicate with students about their progress, and to communicate with parents.

Involve parents. Encourage parents to read to younger children, to provide varied types of high-interest reading materials in the home, to encourage reading, and to ask questions about the students' reading assignments. Discuss the significance of reading with parents, indicate the types of materials that students will be reading in school, and elicit the parents' cooperation as allies in supporting the students' efforts to read. Remind parents that they or other family members can help their children become better readers in English by reading to them in their native language.

Different Students, Different Approaches

Most of the suggestions we have offered in this chapter are as applicable to reading for native-English-speaking students as they are for ESL students. In general we agree with other researchers who have found that instructional processes in reading are similar for both native- and second-language learners (Allen, 1989; Goodman, 1986; Hudelson, 1989; Urzua, 1989). However, teachers may need to employ a broader variety of instructional procedures with ESL learners than would be necessary with native-English speakers and to combine components of this repertoire of practices in creative ways to meet the diverse needs of students who are learning English.

The following differences in teaching reading to ESL students relative to native-English speakers need to be considered:

1. While the reading process may be similar in both groups, greater cognitive demands are made on ESL students, who must develop reading skills simultaneously with oral language skills.

2. No assumptions can be made about homogeneous background of students. Not only may ESL students be of different ages and language backgrounds, but they may have completely different educational backgrounds as well.

3. No single instructional approach is likely to meet all the needs of such a diverse group of students. Instructional approaches need to be adapted to meet students' varied instructional needs.

4. In the case of ESL students, elaboration on or activation of prior knowledge about a topic involves identification and understanding of students' cultural background and experiences.

5. With older ESL students, teachers should capitalize on their level of cognitive maturity rather than using teaching procedures designed for primary-grade students. For example, older students should be more capable of developing metacognitive awareness of reading tasks than younger students.

6. Learning-strategy instruction is especially important in teaching reading to ESL students. Learning strategies can provide ESL students with valuable tools to make use of their prior knowledge, regulate their own learning, and assist their comprehension. Students literate in their native language may not automatically transfer reading strategies to English, and preliterate students need strategy instruction in order to move from a bottom-up to an interactive approach to reading.

7. The definition of "authentic text" needs to extend beyond literature to include all types of texts that students encounter inside and outside school, including content texts and occupationally relevant texts.

8. Literacy instruction, particularly with students in the intermediate grades and up, can begin with the reading of materials in mathematics or science, both of which can be presented with highly contextualized language through visuals, realia, and demonstrations. The students' initial success in recognizing and using authentic content area materials can provide strong motivation for further reading activities.

While approaches to ESL reading for the most part focus on language arts themes and literature, Chamot and O'Malley (1986, 1987, 1989, 1994), Crandall (1987), Hudelson (1989), Mohan (1986), O'Malley and Chamot (1990), and Spanos (1990) suggest content area reading as a vehicle for developing a range of academic-language skills. We believe that ESL instruction is moving in the direction of greater integration of language and content and that the development of academic-language proficiency will become the major objective of ESL instruction in schools. We also believe that teachers will increasingly use alternative assessment with students learning English and will make instructional decisions based on portfolios that enable the teacher to integrate formal and informal information on student progress.

We would like to see empirical evidence on the effectiveness of different approaches and teaching procedures in reading instruction for ESL students before we conclude that any particular approach is superior for ESL students of all ages and types of educational backgrounds. Specific interventions tailored to manipulate variables that are expected to influence student learning in interaction with other variables need to be conducted, as they have been with native-English speakers instructed in strategies such as reciprocal teaching, metacognitive awareness, elaboration, awareness of text organization, and cooperative learning. Furthermore, studies are needed of the transfer of reading strategies from the native language into English in order to determine how best to aid students with literacy skills. And finally, investigation of instructional approaches for students who do not possess literacy skills in their native language should enable us to meet their needs more effectively.

References

Allen, V.G. (1989). Literature as a support to language acquisition. In P. Rigg & V.G. Allen (Eds.), *When they don't all speak English: Integrating the ESL student into the regular classroom.* Urbana, IL: National Council of Teachers of English.

Brinton, D.M., Snow, M.A., & Wesche, M.B. (1989). *Content-based second language instruction.* New York: Newbury.

Brown, A.L., Armbruster, B.B., & Baker, L. (1986). The role of metacognition in reading and studying. In J. Orasanu (Ed.), *Reading comprehension: From research to practice* (pp. 49–75). Hillsdale, NJ: Erlbaum.

Brown, A.L., Bransford, J.D., Ferrara, R.A., & Campione, J.C. (1983). Learning, remembering, and understanding. In J.H. Flavell & M. Markman (Eds.), *Carmichael's manual of child psychology* (vol. 3, pp. 77–166). New York: Wiley.

Brown, A.L., & Palincsar, A.S. (1982). Inducing strategies learning from texts by means of informed, self-control training. *Topics in Learning and Learning Disabilities, 2,* 1–17.

Canale, M., & Swain, M. (1980). Theoretical bases of communicative approaches to second language teaching and testing. *Applied Linguistics, 1,* 1–47.

Carrell, P.L., Devine, J., & Eskey, D.E., (Eds.). (1988). *Interactive approaches to second language reading.* New York: Cambridge University Press.

Chamot, A.U., & O'Malley, J.M. (1986). *A cognitive academic language learning approach: An ESL content-based curriculum.* Washington, DC: National Clearinghouse for Bilingual Education.

Chamot, A.U., & O'Malley, J.M. (1987). The cognitive academic language learning approach: A bridge to the mainstream. *TESOL Quarterly, 21,* 227–249.

Chamot, A.U., & O'Malley, J.M. (1989). The cognitive academic language learning approach. In P. Rigg & V.G. Allen (Eds.), *When they don't all speak English: Integrating the ESL student into the regular classroom.* Urbana, IL: National Council of Teachers of English.

Chamot, A.U., & O'Malley, J.M. (1994). *The CALLA handbook: How to implement the cognitive academic language learning approach.* Reading, MA: Addison-Wesley.

Chamot, A.U., & Stewner-Manzanares, G. (1985). *ESL instructional approaches and underlying language theories.* Washington, DC: National Clearinghouse for Bilingual Education.

Clark, M.A. (1979). Reading in Spanish and English: Evidence from adult ESL students. *Language Learning, 29,* 121–150.

Collier, V.P. (1987). Age and rate of acquisition of second language for academic purposes. *TESOL Quarterly, 21,* 617–641.

Collier, V.P. (1989). How long? A synthesis of research on academic achievement in a second language. *TESOL Quarterly, 23,* 509–531.

Crandall, J.A. (Ed.). (1987). *ESL through content-area instruction: Mathematics, science, social studies.* Englewood Cliffs, NJ: Prentice Hall.

Cummins, J. (1980). Cross-lingual dimensions of language proficiency: Implications for bilingual education and the optimal age issue. *TESOL Quarterly, 14,* 175–187.

Cummins, J. (1984). *Bilingualism and special education: Issues in assessment and pedagogy.* Clevedon, UK: Multilingual Matters.

Derry, S.J. (1990). Learning strategies for acquiring useful knowledge. In B.F. Jones & L. Idol (Eds.), *Dimensions of thinking and cognitive instruction.* Hillsdale, NJ: Erlbaum.

Enright, D.S., & McCloskey, M.L. (1988). *Integrating English: Developing English language and literacy in the multilingual classroom.* Reading, MA: Addison-Wesley.

Freeman, D., Freeman, Y., & Gonzalez, G. (1987). Success for LEP students: The Sunnyside sheltered English program. *TESOL Quarterly, 21,* 361–367.

Garner, R. (1987). *Metacognition and reading comprehension.* Norwood, NJ: Ablex.

Goodman, K. (1986). *What's whole in whole language?* Portsmouth, NH: Heinemann.

Hammerly, H. (1991). *Fluency and accuracy: Toward balance in language teaching and learning.* Clevedon, UK: Multilingual Matters.

Hudelson, S. (1989). "Teaching" English through content-area activities. In P. Rigg & V.G. Allen (Eds.), *When they don't all speak English: Integrating the ESL student into the regular classroom.* Urbana, IL: National Council of Teachers of English.

Jones, B.F., Palincsar, A.S., Ogle, D.S., & Carr, E.G. (1987). *Strategic teaching and learning: Cognitive instruction in the content areas.* Alexandria, VA: Association for Supervision and Curriculum Development.

Krashen, S.D. (1982). *Second language acquisition and second language learning.* Oxford, UK: Pergamon.

Krashen, S.D. (1985). *Input in second language acquisition.* Oxford, UK: Pergamon.

Krashen, S. & Biber, D. (1988). *On course: Bilingual education's success in California.* Sacramento, CA: California Association for Bilingual Education.

Krashen, S.D., & Terrell, T.D. (1983). *The natural approach.* San Francisco, CA: Alemany.

McLaughlin, B. (1987). Reading in a second language: Studies with adult and child learners. In S.R. Goldman & H.T. Trueba (Eds.), *Becoming literate in English as a second language* (pp. 57–70). Norwood, NJ: Ablex.

Mohan, B.A. (1986). *Language and content.* Reading, MA: Addison-Wesley.

National Clearinghouse for Bilingual Education. (1987). Sheltered English: An approach to content area instruction for limited-English-proficient students. *Forum, 10,* 1, 3.

Nattinger, J.R. (1984). Communicative Language Teaching: A new metaphor. *TESOL Quarterly, 18,* 391–407.

Northcutt, L., & Watson, D. (1986). S.E.T.: Sheltered English teaching handbook. Carlsbad, CA: Northcutt, Watson, Gonzalez.

O'Malley, J.M. (1988). The cognitive academic language learning approach (CALLA). *Journal of Multilingual and Multicultural Development, 9,* 43–60.

O'Malley, J.M. (1991, September). *Looking for academic language proficiency.* Paper presented at the National Research Symposium on Limited English Proficient (LEP) Students: Focus on Evaluation and Measurement, Washington, DC.

O'Malley, J.M., & Chamot, A.U. (1990). *Learning strategies in second language acquisition.* New York: Cambridge University Press.

O'Malley, J.M., Chamot, A.U., & Walker, C. (1987). Some implications of cognitive theory for second language acquisition. *Studies in Second Language Acquisition, 9,* 287–306.

Ovando, C.J., & Collier, V.P. (1985). *Bilingual and ESL classrooms: Teaching in multicultural contexts.* New York: McGraw-Hill.

Palincsar, A.S., & Brown, A.L. (1984). Reciprocal teaching of comprehension-fostering and comprehension-monitoring activities. *Cognition and Instruction, 1,* 117–175.

Palincsar, A.S., & Brown, A.L. 1986. Interactive teaching to promote independent learning from text. *The Reading Teacher, 39,* 771–777.

Paris, S.G., & Winograd, P. (1990). How metacognition can promote academic learning and instruction. In B.F. Jones & L. Idol (Eds.), *Dimensions of thinking and cognitive instruction.* Hillsdale, NJ: Erlbaum.

Pressley, M. (1988, June). *Overview of cognitive and metacognitive theories as they relate to special education populations and findings of pertinent intervention research.* Paper presented at Publishers' Workshop, Washington, DC. (Available from Information Center for Special Education Media and Materials, LINC Resources, Inc., Columbus, OH.)

Richards, J.C., & Rodgers, T.S. (1986). *Approaches and methods in language teaching.* New York: Cambridge University Press.

Rigg, P. (1989). Language experience approach: Reading naturally. In P. Rigg & V.G. Allen (Eds.), *When they don't all speak English: Integrating the ESL student into the regular classroom.* Urbana, IL: National Council of Teachers of English.

Savignon, S.J. (1983). *Communicative competence: Theory and classroom practice.* Reading, MA: Addison-Wesley.

Snow, M.E., Met, M., & Genesee, F. (1989). A conceptual framework for the integration of language and content in second/foreign language instruction. *TESOL Quarterly, 23,* 553–574.

Spanos, G. (1990). On the integration of language and content instruction. *Annual Review of Applied Linguistics, 10,* 227–240.

Terrell, T.D. (1981). The Natural Approach in bilingual education. In *Schooling and language minority students: A theoretical framework*. Los Angeles, CA: California State University, Evaluation, Dissemination, and Assessment Center.

Urzua, C. (1989). I grow for a living. In P. Rigg & V.G. Allen (Eds.), *When they don't all speak English: Integrating the ESL student into the regular classroom*. Urbana, IL: National Council of Teachers of English.

Weinstein, C.E., & Mayer, R.E. (1986). The teaching of learning strategies. In M.R. Wittrock (Ed.), *Handbook of research on teaching* (3rd ed., pp. 315–327). New York: Macmillan.

Wilkins, D.A. (1976). *Notional syllabuses*. London: Oxford University Press.

Virginia Garibaldi Allen

6

Selecting Materials for the Reading Instruction of ESL Children

Providing appropriate materials for the reading instruction of ESL children is a difficult task. Decisions must be based on the answers to two broad questions: What does it mean to be literate in the fullest sense of that word? What are the specific and particular considerations that must be given to the child who is faced with both acquiring English as a second language and taking on literacy? It is only after we have answered these questions and others related to them that we can begin to examine the kinds of materials that will support ESL learners as they move into literacy in their second language.

What Is a Literate Person?

There is strong agreement that literacy means far more than being able to encode or decode words. A literate person is not simply one who can read and write, but one who finds pleasure in books and reads and writes for a variety of purposes. Heath (1984) says that to be literate one must go beyond simply getting the main ideas from a text. A literate person, she believes, has the ability to talk and write about language, to explain and put into sequence implicit knowledge and rules of planning, and to speak and write for many purposes in appropriate forms. If teachers are to help children become literate they must ensure that their students develop understanding of the true purposes of reading and writing and engage in authentic reading and writing activities. Materials for reading instruction should encourage children to choose to read, help children discover the values and functions of written language, and permit children to use written language appropriately for a wide range of purposes.

Who Is the ESL Student?

"ESL student" is not a very helpful label. These students have only one similarity—they all need to acquire English as a new language. The range of differences among these children is vast. For example, many southeast Asian immigrants to the United States and Canada have spent a large part of their childhood in refugee camps and have had meager educational experiences. Some groups, such as the Hmong, do not have a cultural heritage of literacy. On the other hand, there are now many Japanese students attending U.S. schools while their parents are on assignment in the United States. These children arrive with a solid educational background, and most continue Japanese studies while attending U.S. schools, because they will be returning to Japan to complete their education. In addition, ESL children enter school with great differences in their exposure to the English language. Immigrant groups such as the Russian Jews may have their first opportunity to hear English only when they reach their new country. In contrast, many children in the United States whose home language is Spanish have lived in the country for some time, are surrounded by English, and have acquired aspects of English from television, in shops, and on playgrounds. The range of ages of ESL students also has to be considered. While many enter school at age five or six, many others arrive in U.S. and Canadian schools at junior and senior high school age.

Materials for reading instruction must support children who are just beginning to speak English, as well as those who already have a limited command of some aspects of the language. They must be appropriate for the age and interest level of the children. Further, they must be chosen with knowledge of the children's cultural background.

In Which Language Should Literacy Begin?

All children moving into literacy must make the connection between oral language and written language. Second-language learners may find that connection difficult when reading and writing instruction is begun in a language that they do not yet speak with any ease. Therefore, a major issue continues to be whether ESL children should be taught to read and write in their own language or whether they should begin the process in English. Common sense would suggest that if children begin to learn about reading and writing in a language they already control, they can draw upon their knowledge of the sounds, structures and meaning of that language as they move into print (Goodman, Goodman, & Flores, 1979; Hudelson, 1987). However, resources may be limited for some groups of second language learners. Few teachers are fluent speakers of less commonly taught languages such as Arabic or Vietnamese. Whereas a rich array of materials is available in Spanish, materials in languages such as Hmong, Arabic, or Navaho may be difficult to find. Therefore, many ESL children will be learning to read and write at the same time as they are acquiring their new language. When possible, however, books and materials in the child's native language should be a part of the literacy program. Materials in English should be selected in order to help the child acquire English along with literacy.

What Special Considerations Need to Be Given to the ESL Student?

All children hypothesize, test and revise their understanding of written language in ways that are similar to the steps they go through in their development of oral language (Bissex, 1980; Goodman, 1967; Read, 1975; Smith, 1971). They draw on the print environment that surrounds them, and even before formal schooling they are beginning to make sense of the written language system (Harste, Woodward, & Burke, 1984).

For many ESL students, opportunities to interact with print in English are few, if they exist at all. Second-language learners frequently draw on their knowledge of print in their first language as they begin to read and write in English. All ESL children need a strong print environment in English and, if possible, in their native language if they are to master the written language system. Hudelson's (1984) examination of the writing of Hispanic children led her to conclude that ESL children should be encouraged to explore writing in English even before they have control of the oral aspects of their new language. She found that the children in her study used Spanish to help them fill in what they could not yet express in English.

The prior knowledge that one brings to a reading selection greatly determines how well one reads that piece. Children in the United States reading a story about Halloween would immediately think of costumes, masks, trick or treat, and bobbing for apples. Children from other countries and cultures would have no prior knowledge to help them understand these "strange" rituals. Goodman and Goodman (1978) found that children from four different nationality groups, despite their limitations in English, were able to read and retell stories in English. However, the more these children already knew about the content, the easier it was for them to read and understand the text. Reading materials selected for use with ESL children should be examined for the kinds of knowledge readers must have to understand them.

Finally, the structure of the text must be considered. Readability formulas that focus on length of words and sentences and on the frequency of words do not help teachers see the difficulties that may make the selection troublesome for the second-language learner. Rigg (1986) analyzed mis-cues of Southeast Asian children as they read aloud materials that were being used in their classrooms. She found that the story that was read most easily by the children was one that had a familiar folktale structure; the text that created problems was one that shifted back and forth between a narrative and an expository style. The way in which the author organizes the information to be conveyed needs to be considered when reading materials are selected.

What Are the Criteria for Selecting Reading Materials for ESL students?

The preceding discussion suggests certain criteria for selecting reading materials for the ESL student. Materials chosen should do the following:

- encourage children to choose to read;
- help children discover the values and functions of written language;
- permit children to use written language for a wide range of purposes;
- be appropriate for the age and interest level of the children;
- take into account the children's cultural background;
- make use of the children's native languages when possible;
- support the children's acquisition of English;
- offer a rich array of genres;
- have text structures that will support children's understanding; and
- take into consideration the children's background knowledge.

Clearly, the above criteria, wide-ranging and extensive as they are, cannot be met by any single textbook series. In the following section, I will explore children's own written language, "real world" print, commercial text series, and children's literature as valuable reading materials that can be used in the ESL classroom.

Materials to Support ESL Children's Literacy Acquisition

Children's Own Writing

The language experience approach, as espoused by Allen and Allen (1976), Hall (1981), and others and explained in the preceding chapter, allows beginning readers to draw on their own experiences and language as they make connections with written text.

The following language-experience story was written down by a teacher who observed a twelve-year-old Cambodian boy work with great care over several days, creating a picture of the home he had left behind. When she asked him to tell her about the picture, he dictated the following:

> This picture is in Cambodia. I have a small house and behind my house I have a blue mountain and the three mountains. Beside my house there's two coconut and one tree behind the house. Behind my house I have a small rice field. It just grows. In front of my house I have a small lake and in the lake it have some flower they call lily. In front of the rice field there's the path to walk. In the mountain there's many bird flying to another tree. There's clouds in the sky.
>
> My house is made by wood and it have two windows and one door. It have eight stilts because I want to keep the animal away. I have the roof on the top of my house. The roof is made by the long grass. It's good grass.

The teacher was astounded by the flow of language from this normally reticent child. The author read his story aloud to the whole class, and it was typed and bound into a book that was read and reread by other students.

A few examples of other ways of making children's own language part of the classroom reading material are (1) charts of words the children are learning as they explore a specific topic, (2) class books that tell of shared experiences such as a field trip, (3) labels to explain a classroom exhibit, (4) written accompaniments to a bulletin-board display of children's artwork, and, (5) individual books made by children on topics of their own choosing, bound and made available to the class. Such materials develop a strong, supportive print environment on which children can draw as they move into literacy.

The use of children's own writing as a part of the reading program meets the following criteria:

- It permits children to use written language for a wide range of purposes.
- It is appropriate for the age and interest level of the children.
- It takes into account the children's cultural backgrounds.
- It can make use of the children's native languages.
- It draws on children's background knowledge.

"Real World" Print

It is clear that young children make use of the environmental print that surrounds them. Even before they enter a classroom, many have begun to make sense out of some of the written language around them (Harste, Burke & Woodward, 1982). Many can read the *Stop* sign and the *In* and *Out* signs on doors, and can point out the name of their favorite fast-food restaurant. Second-language learners do the same thing, so it is vital that their classrooms provide a rich input of print. In addition to the children's own writing, teachers can make available what I call *real world* print.

Newspapers, magazines, brochures, catalogs, posters, letters, menus, and even job applications can provide myriad purposes for exploring print. Young children may peruse the advertisements in a newspaper to find names of foods they know. Older children may look at the Help Wanted section to see what types of jobs are being advertised. Menus from local restaurants can be a part of role-playing and can allow children to compare prices, discover how food offerings are grouped, and compare and contrast menus for fast-food eateries, ethnic restaurants, and elegant dining places. Seed packets, recipes, and game directions provide authentic reasons for careful reading.

When ESL teachers make such print available and help children develop the strategies to read it, they are assisting the children to develop the skills they need to make sense of all the print around them. Indeed, they are opening the door to independence in literacy acquisition. The thoughtful use of a wide range of real world materials encourages children to choose to read for a variety of purposes, and helps them discover the values and functions of written language.

Textbooks

Basal readers. In many schools, basal readers are central to the reading program. Basal reader series include graded sets of reading selections, workbooks, tests, and teachers' manuals. Vocabulary in the reading passages is controlled. The approach to reading instruction is usually eclectic. There is a focus on developing specific word-analysis skills, as well as a sight vocabulary.

With ESL children, these materials should be used selectively and with great care. The very things that the developers of basal readers do in order to make learning how to read easier may make it more difficult for the ESL child. For example, controlling the vocabulary by focusing on high frequency words and words that have phonic regularity may make it extremely difficult for the ESL child to predict what the text will say.

Since basal readers are designed for the child whose first language is English, teachers need to consider the prior knowledge a child would require in order to understand the selection. For example, a story about a school baseball game, while appealing to the interests of many North American children, might be very confusing to a child from another culture. As the teacher examines the reading selection, consideration needs to be given to vocabulary items that might pose problems. Terms such as *bases, foul ball, innings,* and *home runs,* for instance, would have little meaning for some ESL students, and the concept of school rivalry does not exist in all cultures. Figurative language can also be quite confusing. Illustrations should also be examined to ascertain whether they will help the ESL child extract meaning from the text. Finally, while basal readers are designed both to sequence and pace reading instruction, that sequence and pace may be inappropriate for the ESL child. For example, 10-year-old second-language learners given a primer because of their limited proficiency in English, might find the interest level of the book quite different from their own.

If the criteria for materials selection for ESL reading listed earlier in this chapter are to be met, teachers will need to use basal readers selectively, choosing stories that are appropriate for the ESL child and skipping over ones that are not. In order to develop students' prior knowledge, the teacher will need to think of appropriate prereading experiences shaped to the specific needs of the ESL children in the classroom. Workbook pages will need to be examined carefully and used sparingly. Finally, children's literature should provide an extension to the basal program.

Content area textbooks. Content area textbooks are widely used to support such curricular areas as science, health, and social studies. Teachers need to be aware of some specific difficulties these pose for the second-language learner. While basal reader selections are largely in the narrative form, content area texts use other organizational patterns such as time sequence, cause and effect, or compare and contrast. The information load in these texts is often very dense. Vocabulary may be both more precise and more abstract than in basals. For example, a health book may require the reader to understand the exact differences between arteries, veins, and capillaries; a social studies text may assume the understanding of such abstractions as freedom, justice, liberty, and democracy.

Content area texts can, of course, be integrated successfully into ESL learning and teaching. As described in chapter 5, CALLA, or the Cognitive Academic Learning Approach (Chamot & O'Malley, 1986), is designed to help ESL students develop the academic language they need in order to participate in content area classes and to cope with content area materials. The approach provides a framework to assist both ESL and mainstream teachers to meet the specific needs of the ESL student. As with basals, however, content texts should be used carefully and selectively with ESL students, and should be supplemented with other reading material, such as children's literature.

Children's Literature

Children's literature is viewed by many researchers and teachers as the best material for reading instruction (Cullinan, 1989; Huck, 1977). Studies have linked children's language development to their exposure to literature (Chomsky, 1972). Both vocabulary development and syntactic maturity have been found to be influenced positively by reading and listening to stories (Cohen, 1968; Nagy, Herman, & Anderson, 1985).

Elley and Mangubhai (1983) conducted a study of a literature-based reading program with fourth- and fifth-grade second-language learners in 8 rural schools in the Fiji Islands. At the end of 8 months they found that the children using children's literature had shown progress in reading at twice the usual rate. After 20 months they found that these gains had not only continued, but had spread to other related language skills.

Children's books can provide a rich input of cohesive language, made comprehensible by patterned language, predictable structure, and strong, supportive illustrations. Further, these books provide reasons to talk and offer a framework for writing. Good children's books can help move second-language learners into their new language and the world of literacy. However, as with other reading material, literature needs to be selected taking into consideration both its quality and the special needs of the ESL child. Some suggestions for making selections follow, and a list of recommended books from different categories is found at the end of this chapter.

Selecting Books for the Beginning ESL Student

Concept Books

For the child just beginning the move into a new language, one of the first priorities is the acquisition of new labels for old experiences, and for the many new experiences of life in a second culture. Concept books can provide strong support at this point. These books describe the varied dimensions of a single object, a class of objects, or an abstract idea (Huck, Hepler, & Hickman, 1987, p. 173). Descriptions of a few such books follow.

Anne and Harlow Rockwell's *The Toolbox* offers clear and simple pictures of items that might be found in a toolbox: a hammer, a wrench, a screwdriver, and even curly wood shavings. The spare and carefully worded text describes the function of each tool. Tana Hoban has used her great skill as a photographer to create a large number of beautiful picture books that help children focus their attention on a number of significant concepts. These books include *Circles, Triangles and Squares*; *Over, Under, Through, and Other Spatial Concepts*; and *Push Pull, Empty Full: A Book of Opposites*. While Hoban's books are suitable for the young English-speaking child, many of them are appropriate for ESL students of all ages. *Bread, Bread, Bread* by Ann Morris shows bread of all kinds as it is made and eaten around the world. There are photographs of an Arabic father sharing pita bread with his small son, a baker filling a basket with crusty French baguettes, and a Navaho mother preparing fried bread for her family.

Books can also help ESL children categorize knowledge about new experiences. Foods that are commonplace to children in the United States or Canada may be exotic or unknown to the ESL child. Lois Ehlert's *Growing Vegetable Soup* with its bold and colorful pictures lets children watch the growth of plants from seeds to plump vegetables ready to eat. It helps them discover the categories of vegetables that are picked and vegetables that are dug up. It even includes a recipe for vegetable soup.

Some books can link old experiences with new. *People* by Peter Spier examines such concepts as beauty, homes, games, and food as understood by people around the world. For example, the homes shown include the U.S. suburban split-level, the houses on stilts found in southeast Asia, and the tents of the Bedouins, among many others. When I was sharing this book with a young Cambodian boy, he looked up at me with a huge smile, pointed to the house on stilts, and said, "My house!" He then talked about and drew pictures of his old home, surrounded by mountains, streams, and lush vegetation, not at all like his new home in a housing project.

Books With Predictable Features

Peterson (1992), in examining the difficulty level of books for young, at-risk children, identifies factors that make text predictable. They include content as it relates to the background experiences of the child, language patterns, vocabulary, illustration as it supports the meaning of the text, and the narrative style of the book. She points out that a book may be quite appropriate for one child at a particular level but not for another child at the same level. She uses the example of the familiar story of "The Three Little Pigs." A child who has heard this story many times can easily predict what the text will say. The child knows the story events as well as such refrains as "Not by the hair of my chinny, chin, chin." But a second-language learner for whom this story is completely new may have problems tapping into the meaning of the strange happenings. The nonsense words of the refrain may actually interfere with the ESL child's understanding of this tale.

Books such as *The Great Big Enormous Turnip* (Leo Tolstoy) and *The Napping House* (Audrey Wood) are predictable because they are cumulative. Other books, such as *The Three Billy Goats Gruff* (Paul Galdone) or *Titch* (Pat Hutchins) have a predictable pattern of events. Still others, such as *Brown Bear, Brown Bear, What Do You See?* (Bill Martin, Jr.) and *A Dark, Dark Tale* (Ruth Brown) have repetitive language patterns. These books supply cohesive chunks of language that invite children to chime in and read along. They offer repetition in ways that are inviting for English speakers and English learners.

Books Whose Illustrations Support and Extend Meaning

In any good picture book, the illustrations not only convey what is in the text but extend and sharpen the message. In Mirra Ginsberg's *The Chick and the Duckling,* the text tells us that the chick and the duckling went for a walk. The duckling takes the role of leader and says, "I'm taking a walk" and the chick immediately responds, "Me, too." The book follows this pattern of statement of action and response of "Me too." However, it is the dramatic and colorful illustrations by José Aruego that not only support the meaning of the text, but add the humor. When the duckling decides to capture a worm and the chick follows his lead, the picture shows us that they are pulling on opposite ends of the same worm. When the duckling decides to swim and the chick follows suit, the picture shows us the chick's frantic struggle to stay afloat. These books extend the ESL child's understanding of the author's message and draw him or her more deeply into the world of the book.

The types of books discussed here are examples of the many books that can support the beginning ESL student because the illustrations and patterned language make the text comprehensible. Such books should be shared by the teacher as part of a planned read-aloud program. ESL children should have many opportunities to do shared reading of such books with an adult or another child. Time should be made for teacher and child to talk together about these books. It is important that the books be made available so that the ESL children can read the ones they enjoy again and again.

For ESL children who are beyond the beginning stages, books need to be selected that will help them become fluent readers who can talk in meaningful ways about what they are reading. They also need to grow as writers. Here, too, books can provide strong support for the many aspects of the writing process. The acquisition of English is, after all, only one of the tasks facing ESL children. They must also acquire the concepts expected of all children in the school setting and the strategies needed to become lifelong learners. Carefully selected books can support the entire curriculum.

Books That Invite Talk

Too frequently, good books are read aloud, then quickly shelved so that the children can get back to the "real work" of the classroom. Yet the opportunity to respond to a book is central to becoming a reflective reader. Often book discussions are viewed as a time for the teacher to ask questions of the children to see if they have indeed read the story. However, real book discussions are opportunities for children to express a personal response to reading. Children's responses to literature can allow the teacher to observe the connections that each child is making. K. Smith (1990) tells of one young second-language learner who had been reading in English for only two years. She told her teacher one morning that she had just finished reading *A Taste of Blackberries* by Doris Smith, a book that tells of the sudden death of a young boy. The teacher asked the child what she had experienced. The girl replied that she had cried and then added, "I tasted blackberries once and they were sour, and now I know that death is sour" (p. 29). This response revealed a great deal about the reader and the deep connections she was making with a particular book.

Book comparisons are especially useful because they require children to think about the books from a fresh perspective. Often books with the same theme can be compared. Leo Lionni, for example, has written a number of books that explore the theme of being oneself: *The Biggest House in the World, Fish Is Fish,* and *Frederick.* It is also useful for children to discover how different authors have approached the same topic. The love offered by and given to grandparents is a subject that many writers of books for young children have explored. Tomie dePaola's *Nana Upstairs and Nana Downstairs,* John Burningham's *Grandpa,* and Aliki's *The Two of Them* allow children to talk about their own relationships with grandparents. Cultural differences may also be explored as children think about the roles that grandparents play in their lives.

Thoughtful groupings of books can help second-language learners by providing them with real reasons to talk, as well as the story language input to support that talk. Comparing books with similar themes can help deepen children's comprehension of the texts.

Books That Offer a Framework for Writing

Just as children need to learn to use oral language for a variety of functions, so too they need to be able to use written language appropriately for a wide range of purposes. Books can not only give reasons to write and language to support that writing, they can offer models to frame the written product. Janet and Allan Ahlberg's book *The Jolly Postman* follows a postman on his route. He delivers a note of apology to the three bears' cottage from Goldilocks, a flyer on the latest bargains in witchly products to the Gingerbread House, and a rather threatening letter to the wolf from a legal firm to let him know that he is being sued by the three little pigs. These letters can be taken from their envelopes, which are part of the book. Each letter serves a different function and has a decidedly different form. Because the letters are written by and for characters well known in the folktale world, they allow ESL children, who have often had rich experiences with folktales, to explore letter-writing language and letter-writing conventions.

One essential part of learning new concepts, ideas, and information is being able to organize and express that knowledge. Here too, books can provide powerful models. In George Lyon's *ABCEDAR,* an enormous amount of information about trees is presented in alphabet format. The first page focuses on the aspen tree. Illustrations include pictures of the leaf, the seed, and a silhouette of the tree showing its size as compared to that of a person. Lyon's text is simple and clear. This book gives children a model that will allow them to share similar information on other topics.

Books That Support the Curriculum

In the upper elementary years, the content of the curriculum becomes broader. The major focus shifts from helping children learn to read books to helping them use books to acquire and organize new information. As pointed out earlier, textbooks in areas such as social studies, science, and health can be particularly difficult for ESL children. It is helpful for all students in a classroom to have a large number of books available that supplement and enlarge on the information in textbooks, but for ESL learners this is particularly important.

For example, ESL children in a class studying the human body could gather interesting and significant information from Jonathan Miller's beautifully designed, three-dimensional book *The Human Body.* The book allows children to lift the ribcage to expose the lung, pull a tab to see how the heart valves function, and discover how an image becomes focused on the retina. The new vocabulary, difficult to understand from a glossary definition, becomes clear when demonstrated so explicitly in this book. For ESL children in the United States, stories of pioneer life on the prairie are not a part of their heritage. Pam Conrad's book *Prairie Visions: The Life and Times of Solomon Butcher* can make those days come alive. The text of this book, though fascinating, would be difficult for the second-language learner, but the photographs are magnificent. Solomon Butcher set out with his heavy camera to photograph the pioneers in Nebraska; the reader sees actual sod homes, children playing in the yards, women showing off prized possessions. The opportunity to see real faces makes history come alive in a dramatic way.

What is important here is that children have access to large numbers of books that deal with what they are learning. These books should have a wide range of reading levels and offer children rich resources in photographs, maps, diagrams, and drawings that will support the goals of the program of studies.

Books Linked to ESL Children's Cultures

It is important to have books in the classroom library that relate to ESL children's own culture. Not only does it help the self-esteem of the ESL children, it also supports the growth of the other children's awareness of and respect for the cultural groups that make up their society.

Folklore, songs, and poetry, as well as information books, can offer much to ESL children and other children alike. One group of books is of particular interest. Series editor Harriet Rohmer has selected authentic folktales from many cultures. These stories are published as bilingual texts with illustrations that share the artforms of the culture in colorful and exciting ways. Tran-Khan-Tuyet's version of *The Little Weaver of Thai-Yen Village* is in English and Vietnamese, Min Paek's *Aekyung's Dream* is in English and Korean, and Rohmer's adaptation of *Uncle Nacho's Hat* is in English and Spanish. This series continues to grow.

In selecting books about the ESL child's first culture, it is important to avoid those that show stereotyped views. One book cannot cover everything, but if children are able to explore a wide range of books about the culture, they should emerge with not only the folklore and cultural heritage, but a view of the range of differences that exist in the contemporary life of people in that part of the world. It is useful for children to focus on things that are alike across cultures, as well as on the differences. In Florence Heide's *The Day of Ahmed's Secret* we follow a young Egyptian boy as he makes his way through Cairo's alleys and outdoor markets, down busy streets filled with cars and carts, buses and camels. All day long he holds his secret, longing for the moment when he can share it with his family. Finally he arrives at his warm, loving home and tells his special secret: "Look, I can write my name," he says, and he holds up a piece of paper with his name written in Arabic. While the setting and the alphabet are specific, the experience and the emotions are common to all.

Choosing Materials, Using Them Well

In this chapter I have proposed criteria for selecting reading materials for ESL children and discussed a variety of materials that meet those criteria. It is clear that no one set of materials, however well intentioned their selection, will be able to meet the wide range of needs of this special population of children. It is also clear that by drawing wisely on a well-selected mix of materials, teachers can support the literacy development of ESL children within the framework of the regular classroom, for the criteria proposed are valid for materials selection for English-speaking children as well.

What is important to remember is that a good collection of books is not enough, no matter how well selected they are. Books need to be read and used appropriately. The teacher's role goes beyond making thoughtful selections. First and foremost it requires that teachers provide time for children to choose, read, and talk together about books. It further includes (1) matching books with particular children to meet both their language needs and their interests, (2) selecting books that support vocabulary development, (3) exploring how books can help children develop specific aspects of oral and written language, (4) choosing books that support understanding across the curriculum, (5) helping children revisit books in significant ways, (6) using books to support talk in book discussions and conferences, (7) thinking of ways that books can be a springboard to writing for a variety of purposes, and (8) using children's responses to books as one way of assessing children's developing language and literacy.

If reading materials are used in these ways, they will allow teachers to meet the individual needs of ESL children and at the same time to integrate the program of the ESL child with the ongoing work of the classroom.

References

Allen, R.V., & Allen, C. (1976). *Language experiences in reading.* Chicago, IL: Encyclopedia Britannica.

Bissex, G.L. (1980). *GYNS AT WRK: A child learns to read and write.* Cambridge, MA: Harvard University Press.

Chamot, A.U., & O'Malley, J.M. (1986). *A Cognitive Academic Learning Approach: An ESL content-based curriculum.* Washington, DC: National Clearinghouse for Bilingual Education.

Chomsky, C. (1972). Stages in language development and reading exposure. *Harvard Educational Review, 42,* 1–33.

Cohen, D. (1968). The effect of literature on vocabulary and reading achievement. *Elementary English, 45,* 209–213, 217.

Cullinan, B.E. (1989). *Literature and the child* (2nd ed.). San Diego, CA: Harcourt Brace.

Elley, W.B., & Mangubhai, F. (1983). The impact of reading on second language learning. *Reading Research Quarterly, 19,* 53–67.

Goodman, K. (1967). Reading: A psycholinguistic guessing game. *Journal of the Reading Specialist, 6,* 126–135.

Goodman, K., & Goodman, Y.M. (1978). *Reading of American children whose language is a stable rural dialect or a language other than English* (NIE-C-00-3-0087). Washington, DC: U.S. Department of Health, Education, and Welfare.

Goodman, K., Goodman, Y.M., & Flores, B. (1979). *Reading in the bilingual classroom: Literacy and biliteracy.* Rosslyn, VA: National Clearinghouse for Bilingual Education.

Hall, M.A. (1981). *Teaching reading as language experience.* Columbus, OH: Merrill.

Harste, J., Burke, C., & Woodward, V. (1982). Children's language and world: Initial encounters with print. In J.A. Langer & M.T. Smith-Burke (Eds.), *Reader meets author/Bridging the gap.* Newark, DE: International Reading Association.

Harste, J., Woodward, V., & Burke, C. (1984). *Language stories and literacy lessons.* Portsmouth, NH: Heinemann.

Heath, S.B. (1984). Literacy or literate skills? Considerations for ESL/EFL learners. In P. Larson, E.L. Judd, & D.S. Messerschmitt (Eds.), *On TESOL '84: A brave new world for TESOL* (pp. 15–28). Washington, DC: Teachers of English to Speakers of Other Languages.

Huck, C. (1977). Literature as the content of reading. *Theory into Practice, 16,* 363–371.

Huck, C., Hepler, S., & Hickman, J. (1987). *Children's literature in the elementary school* (4th ed.). New York: Holt, Rinehart.

Hudelson, S. (1984). Kan yu rayt en Ingles: Children become literate in English as a second language. *TESOL Quarterly, 18,* 221-238.

Hudelson, S. (1987). The role of native language in the education of language minority children. *Language Arts, 64,* 827-841.

Nagy, W.E., Herman, P.A., & Anderson, R.C. (1985). Learning words in context. *Reading Research Quarterly, 20,* 233–253.

Peterson, B. (1992). Selecting books for beginning readers. In D.E. DeFord, G.S. Pinnell, & C. Lyons (Eds.), *Bridges to literacy.* Portsmouth, NH: Heinemann.

Read, C. (1975). *Children's categorization of speech sounds in English* (Research Rep. No. 17). Urbana, IL: National Council of Teachers of English.

Rigg, P. (1986). Reading in ESL: Learning from kids. In P. Rigg & D.S. Enright (Eds.). *Children and ESL: Integrating perspectives* (pp. 55–92). Washington, DC: Teachers of English to Speakers of Other Languages.

Smith, F. (1971). *Understanding reading: A psycholinguistic analysis of reading and learning to read.* New York: Holt, Rinehart.

Smith, K. (1990). Entertaining a text: A reciprocal process. In K. Short & C. Pierce (Eds.), *Talking about books,* (pp. 17–31). Portsmouth, NH: Heinemann.

Appendix: Some Recommended Children's Books

Books to Help Young Second-Language Learners Acquire English

Concept Books

Ehlert, L. (1987). *Growing vegetable soup.* San Diego, CA: Harcourt Brace.

Hennessy, B.G. (1990). *School days.* New York: Viking.

Hoban, T. (1972). *Push pull, empty full: A book of opposites.* New York: Macmillan.

Hoban, T. (1973). *Over, under, through and other spatial concepts.* New York: Macmillan.

Hoban, T. (1974). *Circles, triangles and squares.* New York: Macmillan.

Hoban, T. (1990). *Exactly the opposite.* New York: Greenwillow.

MacCarthy, P. (1990). *Ocean parade: A counting book.* New York: Dial.

Miller, M. (1990). *Who uses this?* New York: Greenwillow.

Morris, A. (1989). *Bread, bread, bread.* New York: Lothrop, Lee, & Shepard.

Rockwell, A., & Rockwell, H. (1971). *The toolbox.* New York: Macmillan.

Spier, P. (1980). *People.* New York: Doubleday.

Books with Predictable Features

Brown, R. (1981). *A dark, dark tale.* New York: Dial.

Carle, E. (1968). *The very hungry caterpillar.* New York: Philomel.

Hellen, N. (1988). *The bus stop.* New York: Orchard.

Hutchins, P. (1971). *Titch.* New York: Macmillan.

Galdone, P. (1973). *The three billy goats gruff.* New York: Seabury.

Ginsberg, M. (1972). *The chick and the duckling.* New York: Macmillan.

Martin, B. (1983). *Brown bear, brown bear, what do you see?* New York: Holt.

Tolstoy, L. (1968). *The great big enormous turnip.* New York: Watts.

Trafuri, N. (1988). *Spots, feathers and curly tails.* New York: Greenwillow.

Ward, C. (1988). *Cookie's week.* New York: Putnam.

Wood, A. (1984). *The napping house.* San Diego, CA: Harcourt Brace.

Books Whose Illustrations Strongly Support Meaning

Hall, D. (1980). *The ox-cart man.* New York: Viking.

Hutchins, P. (1982). *One hunter.* New York: Greenwillow.

Hutchins, P. (1968). *Rosie's walk.* New York: Macmillan.

Jonas, A. (1987). *Color dance.* New York: Greenwillow.

Weisner, D. (1991). *Tuesday.* New York: Clarion.

Books to Support the Older ESL Child in Acquiring Literacy

Books That Give a Framework for Writing

Ahlberg, J., & Ahlberg, A. (1986). *The jolly postman or other people's letters.* Boston, MA: Little, Brown.

Brown, M.W. (1949). *The important book.* New York: Harper.

Hunt, J. (1989). *Illuminations.* New York: Bradbury.

Lyon, G. (1989). *ABCEDAR.* New York: Watts.

Van Allsburg, C. (1987). *The z was zapped.* Boston, MA: Houghton Mifflin.

Williams, V., & Williams, J. (1988). *Stringbean's trip to the shining sea.* New York: Greenwillow.

Books to Support the Curriculum

Aliki. (1981). *Digging up dinosaurs.* New York: Crowell.

Byam, M. (1988). *Arms and armor.* New York: Knopf.

Conrad, P. (1991). *Prairie visions: The life and times of Solomon Butcher.* New York: Harper.

Gibbons, G. (1987). *Dinosaurs.* New York: Holiday House.

Goodall, J. (1978). *The story of an English village.* New York: Macmillan.

Hopkins, L. B. (1987). *Dinosaurs.* San Diego, CA: Harcourt Brace.

Lasker, J. (1976). *Merry ever after: The story of two medieval weddings.* New York: Viking.

Macaulay, D. (1973). *Cathedral.* Boston, MA: Houghton Mifflin.

Miller, J. (1983). *The human body.* New York: Viking.

Most, B. (1987). *Dinosaur Cousins.* San Diego, CA: Harcourt Brace.

Wilkinson, P. (1993). *Amazing buildings.* New York: Dorling Kindersley.

Books to Compare and Contrast
- Books on the Same Topic: Grandparents

Aliki (1979). *The two of them.* New York: Greenwillow.

Burningham, J. (1985). *Grandpa.* New York: Crown.

dePaola, T. (1978). *Nana upstairs and Nana downstairs.* New York: Penguin.

- Books by One Author or Books with Similar Themes

Lionni, L. (1969). *The biggest house in the world.* New York: Pantheon.

Lionni, L. (1967). *Frederick.* New York: Pantheon.

Lionni, L. (1970). *Fish is fish.* New York: Pantheon.

- Folktale Variants: "Cinderella"

Clark, A., (1979). *In the land of small dragon.* New York: Viking. (Vietnamese)

Climo, S. (1993). *The Korean Cinderella.* New York: HarperCollins.

Louie, A.-L. (1981). *Yeh Shen: A Cinderella story from China.* New York: Philomel.

Martin, R., & Shannon, D. (1992). *The rough-face girl.* New York: Putnam. (Algonquin)

Phumla. (1972). *Nomi and the magic fish: A story from Africa.* New York: Doubleday.

Books for All Children

Books to Explore Cultural Heritages

Clark, A.N. (1979). *In the land of small dragon.* New York: Viking. (Vietnam)

Delacre, L. (1989). *Arroz con leche.* New York: Scholastic. (Puerto Rico)

Garland, S. (1993). *Why ducks sleep on one leg.* New York:

Scholastic. (Vietnam)

Griego, M., Bucks, B., Gilbert, S., & Kimball, L. (1981). *Tortillitas para mama and other Spanish nursery rhymes*. New York: Holt, Rinehart. (Mexico)

Heide, F. (1990). *The day of Ahmed's secret*. New York: Lothrop, Lee & Shepard. (Egypt)

Paek, N. (1988). *Aekyung's dream* (in English and Korean). San Francisco, CA: Children's Book Press.

Rohmer, H. (Adapter). (1989). *Uncle Nacho's hat: A folktale from Nicaragua,* (in English and Spanish). San Francisco, CA: Children's Book Press.

Tran-Khan-Tuyet (Reviser & Editor). (1988). *The little weaver of Thai-Yen village* (in English and Vietnamese). San Francisco, CA: Children's Book Press.

Books That Look at Cultures Side by Side

Dorros, A. (1991). *Abuela*. New York: Dutton.

Hoyt-Goldsmith, D. (1992). *Hoang Anh: A Vietnamese-American boy*. New York: Holiday House.

Lankford, M. (1992). *Hopscotch round the world*. New York: Morrow.

Levine, E. (1989). *I hate English*. New York: Scholastic.

Lord, B.B. (1983). *In the year of the boar and Jackie Robinson*. New York: Harper.

Morris, A. (1989). *Houses and homes*. New York: Lothrop, Lee & Shepard.

Petit, J. (1983). *My name is San Ho*. New York: Scholastic.

Books to Help People Think about the Immigrant and Refugee Experience

Bunting, E. (1988). *How many days to America?* New York: Clarion.

Garland, S. (1992). *Song of the buffalo boy,* Harcourt, Brace.

Garland, S. (1993). *The lotus seed*. San Diego, CA: Harcourt Brace.

Nodar, C.M. (1992). *Abuelita's paradise*. Morton Grove, IL: Albert Whitman.

Say, A. (1993). *Grandfather's journey*. Boston, MA: Houghton Mifflin.

Whelan, G. (1992). *Goodbye, Vietnam*. New York: Knopf.

Section 3

Instructional Practices

Having considered background issues and organizational concerns that affect the delivery of instruction to ESL students, we now turn to the implementation of effective instructional practices. Our decision to begin this section by focusing on the reading-writing connection reflects insights from recent research about the learning that comes from interrelating reading and writing. These insights support the view that reading and writing are similar processes of meaning construction and that there are many parallels between what readers and writers do. Chapter 7 discusses ways in which teachers can use reading and writing processes to foster the literacy development of their ESL students.

Chapter 8 considers the special ways in which language proficiency and literacy development influence ESL students' access to core curricula. Unfortunately, the academic language and expository texts characteristic of content areas often act as barriers to the success of ESL students. In order to ensure that ESL students have equal access and keep pace with their native-English-speaking classmates in the mastery of content concepts, teachers must be able to implement instructional strategies that facilitate their ESL students' understanding of academic language and their comprehension of expository text.

Chapter 9 concludes this section by addressing one of the greatest challenges educators face: assessing the literacy development of ESL students in a valid and reliable manner. We believe that informal, authentic approaches that integrate instruction and assessment provide the most viable means of identifying student needs, enhancing student learning, and measuring student progress.

Nancy Farnan
James Flood
Diane Lapp

7

Comprehending through Reading and Writing: Six Research-Based Instructional Strategies

The changing demographics of schools in the United States and elsewhere require instructional practices that demonstrate awareness of and appreciation for the cultural and linguistic diversity of students. ESL children are expected to learn more than English in their classrooms; they are expected to follow a curriculum, learn content, and use literacy processes to construct meanings. In this chapter we discuss ways in which teachers can foster reading and writing processes in ESL students in order to help them meet these objectives.

Literacy Issues

Language use for human beings is a natural process integral to our physiological, affective, and cognitive well-being. Language is part of our humanness, and it develops naturally in situations that are meaningful (Cummins, 1985;

Krashen, 1985). In education, there is a tendency for children who lack specific experiences in a particular language to be considered illiterate, literally not literate. However, nothing could be further from the truth, for all children come to school with a wealth of experience in a language (Thonis, 1989). Literacy, of which reading and writing are parts, is developmental. All children are somewhere on a literacy continuum, and it is critical that educators take into consideration and build on the vast store of knowledge and experience all children have. There is no point on the continuum that denotes too much literacy or, for that matter, not enough. There are no good or bad places to be, only places informed by children's previous knowledge and construction of literacy concepts. From this perspective, we cease to view children as having deficiencies that must be remediated or gaps that must be filled in. Instead, we determine what they know and can do and build on whatever foundations they have established.

From the time they begin acquiring language in their native tongue, children begin constructing—not learning—literacy understandings. Ferreiro (1990) points out that children build *interpretation systems* about the nature and function of language. She states, "As we have repeatedly tried to demonstrate, these children's theories are not a pale mirror image of what they have been told. The theories are real constructions that, more often than not, seem very strange to our adult way of thinking" (Ferreiro, 1990, p. 14). These constructions are consistent with *interlanguage,* which has been documented and defined by second-language researchers as the developmental stages involved in moving from a first language to a second language (Brown, 1980). Interlanguage theory posits that the errors learners make while learning a second language are primarily developmental in nature and are a direct result of the learners' attempts to construct meaning from the linguistic stimuli surrounding them.

From this perspective, schools must be literacy environments in which children work and play with language in order to continuously test their language hypotheses and construct new and useful understandings. Thus, the teacher's primary responsibility is to create rich learning environments that provide students with stimulating opportunities to test hypotheses about language and to help them take advantage of those opportunities to build language through the integration of listening, speaking, reading, and writing.

Principles of Literacy Development

As we design instruction intended to enhance children's literacy development, the following principles are important to keep in mind:

- literacy in a second language develops as in the first—globally, not linearly, and in a variety of rich contexts (Rigg & Allen, 1989);

- second-language learning takes place best in risk-free environments where students' experiences and contributions are validated (Law & Eckes, 1990);

- language is best learned when it is "whole"—that is, when it is used for real and meaningful purposes (Edelsky, Altwerger, & Flores, 1991); and

- reading and writing are literacy processes through which children construct meaning, using prior knowledge and a variety of strategies that promote and regulate comprehension (Peregoy & Boyle, 1993).

In the remainder of this chapter, we look at the relationships between reading and writing processes and discuss classroom practices that support literacy development for all students, but particularly those who come to school with a first language other than English.

Reading and Writing: Mutually Enhancing Language Processes

There are few areas in educational research where such broad consensus has been found as the relationship between reading and writing. Most experts agree that, although not identical, reading and writing are similar (Mason, 1989; Rosenblatt, 1989; Shanahan, 1990; Squire, 1983) and mutually supportive (Stotsky, 1983) language processes. Furthermore, research findings suggest that the reading and writing processes function similarly for both first- and second-language learners (Grabe, 1991). For example, both rely on the reader's or writer's background knowledge to construct meaning (Anderson & Pearson, 1984; Carrell, 1988; Pritchard, 1990) and both make use of cueing systems (graphic, syntactic, semantic) to allow the reader or writer to predict and confirm meaning (Carson et al., 1990; Cziko, 1978, 1980).

In her informative and thorough review of research on reading and writing relationships, Stotsky (1983) concluded that (1) good writers tend to be better readers than are less able writers, (2) good writers tend to read more frequently and widely and to produce more syntactically complex writings, (3) writing itself does not tend to influence reading comprehension, but when writing is taught for the purpose of enhancing reading, there are significant gains in comprehension and retention of information, and (4) reading experiences have as great an effect on writing as direct instruction in grammar and mechanics.

Other researchers have established additional relationships between reading and writing. Eckhoff (1983) reported that children's writing reflected the syntactic complexity and stylistic features of texts read in their classrooms, in this case either basal readers or whole pieces of literature. Edelsky (1982) found that when writing in a second language, writers call on what they know in their first language. In addition, Carson (1990) noted that reading experiences improved the writing of second-language learners more than grammar instruction or additional writing exercises.

Reading and Writing Practices That Support Comprehension

There seems to be a strong inclination in education to try to find a single style and set of materials that will address the needs of all children. Although we know much about reading and writing processes and their role in comprehension and literacy development, definitive answers and sure-fire strategies are elusive. In response to the question "Can comprehension be taught?" Flood and Lapp (1991) reviewed studies from the 1980s and concluded that "one has to be careful to add 'Comprehension of what, by whom, under what conditions, and for what purposes?'" (p. 734). Piper (1993) says it another way: "Because no single method of teaching *anything* is right for *every* child, it is something of a truism to say that there is no single best way" (p. 323). However, our rich knowledge base tells us that there are many practices grounded in solid theory and research that, when used thoughtfully and in wide variety, work for many teachers at many grade levels with children of diverse backgrounds and experiences (Krapels, 1990; Urzua, 1987). The following six research-based practices have been specifically selected for discussion because each capitalizes on the interactive nature of reading and writing, thus promoting students' comprehension. In addition, each reflects one or more of the principles discussed earlier.

Reading as Preparation for Writing

Second-language learners must have multiple opportunities to become familiar with a language that is new to them. In addition to speaking and listening, reading can serve as a model and as preparation for writing. For students with the requisite levels of language proficiency and conceptual knowledge, reading, listening to, and discussing texts written by experienced writers will help them become better prepared for their own writing (Smith, 1983). Readers engage with writers. Readers notice spellings of words and patterns of language; they reread passages because something was especially interesting or well said;

they notice the rhymes, rhythms, vocabulary, and syntax of language.

Smith (1992) cautions that this type of learning is continuous, spontaneous, and effortless, "requiring no particular attention, conscious motivation, or specific reinforcement" (p. 432), but that it cannot take place when demands on attention are overloaded by a text that is complex and confusing for a reader, as texts often are for second-language learners. Therefore, it is critical that teachers help students make connections with text in ways that support their understanding. Readers' engagement cannot take place when the purpose of reading is to memorize facts or merely to "get through" the text. Learning is not memorization; it is growth and development. Literacy is not a collection of skills accrued through an accumulation of information. As we discussed earlier, literacy involves readers constructing their own understanding; readers must be involved in text in ways that require personal investment and engagement, which in turn provide opportunities for them to construct meanings for what they read (Faltis, 1993). In essence, writer and reader become collaborators in the reading-writing process.

Using predictable books and patterned language. Through lively, predictable books, students of all ages can begin to construct knowledge relating to language, style, vocabulary, and concepts. If stories are tape-recorded, students can listen to them before, during, or after their own readings. Using predictable books for read-alongs not only gives students experience with predicting outcomes, but also offers frameworks of language patterns that can serve as foundations for "original" stories. In Bill Martin Jr's familiar *Brown Bear, Brown Bear, What Do You See?* the answer to his title question is "I see a red bird looking at me," followed on the next page by "Red bird, red bird, what do you see?" and so forth. A first grader begins her own predictable text this way:

> Butterfly, butterfly
> What do you see?
> I see a puppy looking at me.

For students who are less proficient in English, a whole-class activity could center on constructing a similar narrative on chart paper or chalkboard, thereby enhancing the reading-writing connection. Students can move to individual composing as they become thoroughly familiar with predictable books and their structure and narratives. Additional examples of predictable books include Brian Wildsmith's *Cat on the Mat,* Robert Kalan's *Jump, Frog, Jump!,* Ashley Wolff's *Only the Cat Saw,* and Robert Kraus's *Whose Mouse Are You?* (See Cullinan, 1989, for additional suggestions.)

Collections of nursery rhymes from various countries also offer writing in rhyming and rhythmic patterns. Most cultures have similar nursery rhymes that tell tales about animals, nature, and foolish children and adults. Bringing a range of these writings into classrooms supports connections between all children and what they read, and fosters understanding of traditions and customs in other cultures. Demi's *Dragon Kites and Dragonflies* and Robert Wyndham's *Chinese Mother Goose Rhymes* offer Chinese nursery rhymes; N.M. Bodecker translated and illustrated 14 Danish rhymes in *It's Raining, Said John Twaining;* and Margo Griego and her colleagues have collected nursery rhymes from Mexico and other Spanish-speaking countries in *Tortillitas para Mama.* In several of these collections, the works appear in English as well as the original language.

Using reading, writing, and discussion. Teachers can promote students' reading and writing of narratives by having prereading conferences. In these conferences they can introduce vocabulary ("There are some important words in the story we need to talk about") and story elements such as the basic storyline and characterization ("This story is about..."); they can also make certain that students have an adequate store of appropriate prior knowledge, helping them bring what they already know to the material and thus ensuring comprehension. These strategies are particularly critical for second-language learners to strengthen their conceptual development in order to make information and ideas clear and comprehensible.

Discussions can center on story components such as plot, setting, character, conflict, and resolution. Use of the literary terminology is not the issue. Rather, what is important is that students become familiar with these story elements that make up the "story grammar," and then see how they are handled by a variety of authors. Activities using story grammar will provide ESL students with a consistent framework in which to operate after reading a story. Students can meet in small groups to discuss what they have read and to complete a story grammar sheet similar to the one in Figure 1. Students especially enjoy providing such information on an overhead transparency and sharing it with the class. In this way, all students have an opportunity to see how their peers have talked and thought about a reading.

Students can begin their story-writing experiences by rewriting story endings and by writing classic stories such as fairytales from the point of view of another character in the story. This technique is used engagingly in *The True Story of the 3 Little Pigs,* in which Jon Scieszka retells the familiar story from the wolf's perspective.

The point is that, in order to "read like writers, [children] must see themselves as writers" (Smith, 1983, p. 565).

Figure 1
A Story Grammar Sheet

This story is about _____ .

In the story the characters are _____

_____ . The main problem is that

_____ ,

and it ends when _____ .

The teacher's role is to help children see reading as valuable and interesting and writing as worthwhile and possible. Children must have experience reading stories, poems, and letters, and experience writing them. If they begin to see themselves as writers, they will begin to read texts as writers do.

Using multiple texts. Reading also serves as preparation for writing when students are given opportunities to read multiple texts and resources about a topic before and during their writing, thereby building a sufficient repertoire of concepts and vocabulary (Krashen, 1981). These texts should represent a range of difficulty levels to make them useful for students with a range of language proficiencies. In the process of reading, taking notes, and participating in discussion groups on the topic, students have an opportunity to develop facility with relevant vocabulary and to build schemata that will allow them to write with increasing confidence.

In discussion groups of four to six students, the children can take one or two minutes each to share a piece of information about their topics and to respond to questions from others in the group. These groups should be heterogeneous so that students with varying degrees of language proficiency have opportunities to interact with one another. In such situations, classrooms must be places where students help one another and are free to take risks, knowing that if they are having difficulty or make an error, they will only meet with the kindness and interested support that we expect individuals to extend to one another. Only then can such interactions foster students' reading and writing by allowing them to explore their topic orally in what Dwyer (1991) refers to as "a sea of talk."

It is important to keep in mind that text materials that serve as resources should not be so complex that students have difficulty understanding them. Fortunately, many trade books exist that are motivating as well as easy to read. For example, an intermediate grade student from Samoa who is fascinated with sharks and decided to research the

Comprehending through Reading and Writing   **143**

topic and found such books as Don Reed's *Sevengill: The Shark and Me,* which relates the experiences of a diver at a marine park in California, and Helen Sattler's *Sharks, the Super Fish* which illustrates what is known and raises questions about what is not known about these creatures.

Students should be encouraged to write about what they read, keeping a log or journal in which to take notes and respond to what they find most interesting and informative. After they read, write about, and discuss information found in such trade books, as well as in classroom textbooks and other reference materials, and provided that they are given time to develop background knowledge of the topic, students will be able to write an informative and interesting piece that can be shared with others.

Writing as Preparation for Reading

Teachers use quick-writes in classrooms for a variety of purposes: as a brainstorming process before reading or writing, for example, or as an opportunity to synthesize and display ideas during and after reading (see chapter 8). Quick-writes call on students to jot down their ideas on a topic, without worrying unduly about correctness of mechanics. These are often described as writing-to-learn activities, and their effectiveness arises from the nature of writing itself: that is, writing is thinking. In order to write about a subject, students must access and organize ideas. By writing, they will find themselves clarifying certain points, just as they find questions arising when they try to articulate ideas and perspectives.

When students share such writing, teachers are able to see the understanding that their students are developing as well as to identify their misconceptions. Although the relationship between writing and learning is not a straightforward one and depends a great deal on students' prior knowledge, engagement, attitude, purpose, and ability to read and write, using reading and writing (and rereading and rewriting) together provides a way to help students develop their comprehension of text (Peregoy & Boyle, 1993).

For some students, their level of language proficiency might dilute the effectiveness of quick-writes to enhance learning. If this is the case, students can present their ideas orally, while the teacher writes them on the board or overhead transparency. Then, after much discussion during which the teacher records a variety of words and phrases, students can be given opportunities to produce oral and written sentences that synthesize the ideas. Another option is for students to create this synthesis with the entire class in a group composition activity; or, depending on their language proficiency, students can work in small groups.

Writing before reading also helps students access ideas that will facilitate their understanding of narratives. For example, in *Tuck Everlasting,* Natalie Babbitt writes about eternal life, a subject that has fascinated human beings for centuries. Across cultures, various beliefs surround the subjects of death and immortality. Bringing those various perspectives to light through students' experiences and knowledge of their cultures not only helps individual students make connections with the story, but it also brings valuable information to the classroom. In Babbitt's book, appropriate for more proficient ESL learners, the possibility of life everlasting presents a serious dilemma for a young adolescent girl. Before beginning the novel, a teacher might ask students to think and write on the topic "Would you like to live forever?" Having an opportunity to explore their own thoughts relative to the subject and hearing the ideas of others will give the students a perspective on the problem that lies at the heart of this delightful book. Such writing can be kept in journals for later review and discussion by students as their insights grow and develop throughout their reading.

Webbing, Concept Mapping, and Semantic Mapping

We have already discussed the fact that the prior knowledge that individuals, both native and non-native speakers, bring to either a writing or a reading task exerts a powerful influence on their ability to comprehend and to communicate effectively in print. Webbing provides a structure through which students can access and organize information and ideas and can actively connect the known to the new. Research and theory both support webbing as a vehicle for enhancing comprehension and learning (Bromley, 1991). Similar to concept mapping and semantic mapping (Flood & Lapp, 1988) (see chapter 8), webbing provides illustrative material that helps students access, organize, and evaluate their ideas in the context of what they already know and what new information they are encountering. In this way, it functions as what Boyle and Peregoy (1990) refer to as a *literacy scaffold,* a framework that helps students access "the meanings and pleasure of print" (p. 194) and provides multiple cues that they can use to construct meaning. For second language students, the networks of ideas that are captured in webs and concept maps highlight vocabulary and provide a concrete representation of information in a way that illustrates connections between concepts.

For example, before reading a social studies text on farming in the United States, a third grade teacher can begin a web on the chalkboard, soliciting students' prior knowledge about the subject. In the middle of a circle, the teacher writes the word "farm," and on lines radiating out from the circle, the teacher writes words and phrases that students volunteer. It might look like the web shown in Figure 2.

Such a web can also be drawn on butcher paper or an overhead transparency. It can then be saved and used during and after the reading, when students can review it and add to or revise their original conceptions. As students construct the web, they access what they already know and then reevaluate their prior knowledge (with guidance from the teacher) in light of the new information they have gained from the text.

Because many second-language students do not have the same experience as native speakers with the variety of genres and text structures used in English, webs can

Figure 2
A Web of Farming

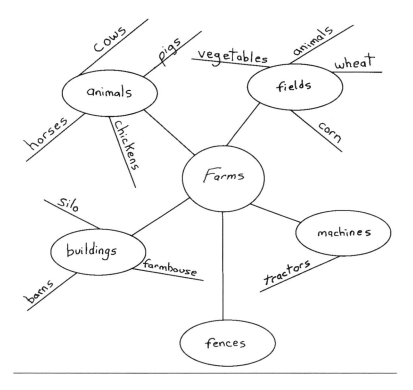

provide opportunities to represent patterns of narrative as well as expository material. For example, one teacher and students constructed a web that illustrates the circular nature of the African folktale *Why Mosquitos Buzz in People's Ears,* told by Verna Aardema). This web (see Figure 3) illustrates a particular story structure which may be unfamiliar to children from diverse language backgrounds.

In the case of expository material, a textbook chapter about the first settlers to arrive on the east coast of the United States might be written in a way that focuses on the problems and hardships that the settlers encountered and the solutions that they were able to devise. As students cre-

Figure 3
Map of Aardema's *Why Mosquitos Buzz in People's Ears*

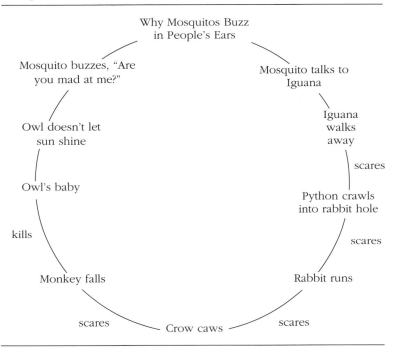

ate webs that illustrate these basic problems and their solutions, they interact purposefully with text, creating a framework that provides support for their comprehension of that particular text structure.

Summarizing

Interest in summarizing as a practice to promote reading comprehension can be traced to studies of the 1920s and 1930s. Salisbury (1934) found that students' comprehension increased when they were made aware of important points in a text before reading and were asked to summarize central concepts in outline form. Kintsch and van Dijk (1978) renewed interest in summarization when their research tied its use to increased comprehension.

Although there is no universal definition for a summary, Annis (1985) described three requirements associated with the summarization process: (1) focused attention on the task, (2) explicit connection of a reader's prior knowledge to material in the text, and (3) the transfer of central ideas in a text into the reader's own words.

Hill (1991) makes the point that students do not know intuitively how to write effective summaries. The task is especially complex for second-language learners because they must negotiate both unfamiliar syntax and unfamiliar vocabulary to achieve comprehension and construct a summary. Hill suggests that teachers direct students to begin with the simplest type of summary: a chronology of events associated with narratives. This is, in essence, a retelling dictated by the simple progression of events in a story; it represents a simpler task than writing a summary of a variety of expository text patterns.

Moving beyond chronology, students can learn to create concept webs, such as those discussed previously, as the next step in summarizing (Hill, 1991). With the webs, students learn to differentiate between main and supporting points; the webs can then be used as organizers for summaries. Through this process, students expand their summary-writing skills beyond a retelling of events. They learn to condense by choosing main points and reorganizing them into summaries for a variety of text structures, such as comparison-contrast, problem-solution, cause-effect, and so forth.

To help students grasp the concept of summarizing, the teacher can model the summarizing process using a variety of materials. For example, as a class reads about and discusses current events reported in the newspaper, the teacher can model his or her thinking in choosing the main ideas from news stories, features, or editorials; then, the teacher can write these ideas on the board and can think aloud while organizing them into a short summary and guiding discussion concerning the final product (see chapter 9). As an alternative or subsequent activity, the teacher can write a summary while the students, alone or in small groups, write a summary of their own. Teacher and students can then compare these summaries, discussing and evaluating effective versus less effective products.

The alternatives are numerous. Which process works well with a particular classroom depends on students' levels of expertise and language proficiency. Through modeling by the teacher, practice, and discussion, students can refine their summary-writing skills and thereby deepen their reading comprehension.

Written Communication: The Morning Message

Classroom practices must foster in children a desire to become literate. In many homes, literacy is taken for granted. Notes left on refrigerators, grocery lists, telephone messages, letters sent and received, and notes between home and school all emphasize the importance of literacy. In these homes, children develop their facility with print naturally. Such communications help children perceive print as a natural and necessary part of their lives, and it is this perception that must be fostered in the classroom for all children.

Many classroom activities can help students develop this view of literacy. One such activity is described in a report by Kawakami-Arakaki, Oshiro, and Farran (1989). In an attempt to integrate reading and writing for the purpose of enhancing reading achievement with at-risk Hawaiian and part-Hawaiian students, several researchers worked in collaboration with teachers to implement what they referred to as the "morning message." This activity gives a fresh slant to typical beginning-of-the-day classroom business and is "deliberately structured to demonstrate the importance of reading and writing in the classroom" (p. 201).

The following is an example of a typical morning message in an elementary classroom early in the school year: after taking attendance, the teacher sits the entire class in a semicircle on the floor and writes on the board, "Today is September 7, 1991. We will listen to music today." This message contains some practical information and an item of interest to the children—that is, they will be listening to music. Then the teacher, asking children to read along, reads the message while pointing to the words. The teacher leads the reading a second time and then engages children in a discussion of the written text. The questions are simple: Who knows what this word is? Who knows a word on the board? What words are alike? What part of the message tells you today's date? As the school year progresses, the complexity of the messages increases and they grow into multiple sentences. The teacher and the students work together to use phonic, syntactic, and semantic cueing systems to develop the messages' meaning. The teacher begins asking students what they notice about each written message. They may point to upper- and lowercase letters, terminal punctuation, contractions, words embedded within words ("day" in "Wednesday," for example), rhymes, or inflectional endings.

With the morning message, a simple business routine becomes an instructional event in this classroom. The practice promotes the development of literacy skills because the teacher designs messages to expand students' awareness of reading and writing processes and their integration. In addition, it highlights the importance of literacy through a message that is authentic and meaningful for students.

Dialogue Journals

It has been well documented that interactions in the classroom are usually quite different from those in the home, on the street corner, or on the playground (Bruner, 1978; Dyson, 1984; Dyson & Freedman, 1991). Most children quickly notice the difference, and for some the transition in language use from home to school can be difficult. For non-native speakers, the transition can be even more confusing, and in their case it is crucial that classroom discourse be real and meaningful. Like the morning message, dialogue journals are structured to cause students to interact with reading and writing, giving them the opportunity to develop a sense of ownership of writing that is highly functional and communicative (Urzua, 1987).

The terms *journal, log, diary,* and *notebook* are used in various ways and at times interchangeably. *Dialogue* journals, however, differ markedly from typical classroom journals or logs. They are written conversations between partners, usually a student and teacher. Each student, regardless of his or her level of English proficiency, writes an entry daily (or perhaps once or twice a week, depending on teacher judgment) to which the teacher responds. If the student does not speak English and the teacher knows the student's first language, the entries can be written in that language. If the teacher is monolingual, parents or a bilingual paraprofessional can assist the student in writing the entry in English. As the students learn English, they can gradually incorporate English into their writing with the assistance of the teacher. Such entries might be only one or two sentences long at first.

The teacher's role is to support children's literacy development and to respond as a conversationalist might, reacting with personal comments, anecdotes, and questions. This should not be a question-answer interaction, but rather a sustained conversation, a transaction between reader, writer, and text, to use Rosenblatt's (1985) terminology. The intent is to involve students in reading and writing processes that are communicative and thus motivational in nature; students choose their own topics, write their entries, and eagerly read the teacher's response. Figure 4 shows a sample entry from a first grade ESL student's journal.

Dialogue journals have been found to be highly effective with second-language students, as well as with native speakers at various stages of literacy development. Studies that have examined the use of dialogue journals report substantial improvement in students' writing, fluency, elaboration of topics, and use of conventional syntax (Kreeft & Shuy, 1985; Staton, et al., 1988). Through such writer-reader transactions, students learn that reading and writing are purposeful and interconnected activities. Dolly

Figure 4
Dialogue Journal

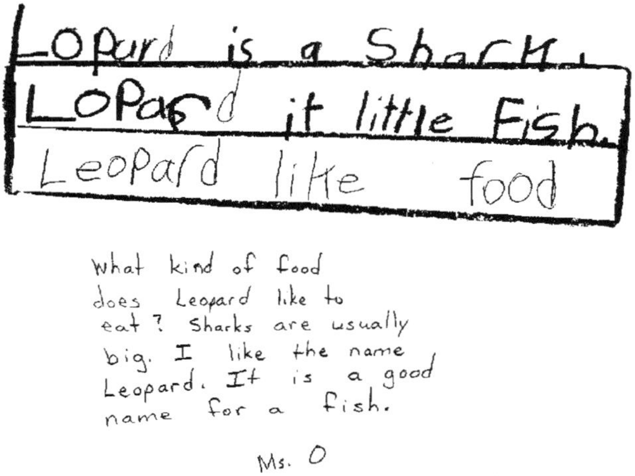

LOpard is a Shark.
LOPard it little Fish.
Leopard like food

What kind of food
does Leopard like to
eat? Sharks are usually
big. I like the name
Leopard. It is a good
name for a fish.

Ms. O

(1990) reported on the success she enjoyed with dialogue journals in her ESL classes: "The dialogue journal can help learners discover that both writing and reading require awareness of and collaboration with others, not merely putting words on paper in a vacuum or absorbing information that has magically appeared on a page" (p. 364).

A Final Note

Teachers must feel empowered to teach all children effectively. Simplistic answers to complex literacy issues do not exist. However, when classroom practices are based on sound theory and research, there is a greater chance that they will be effective for both native and non-native English speakers. When students are actively engaged in authentic, purposeful activities that capture their interest, promote interaction, and facilitate communication, teachers can be assured that the students are well on the road to success in reading and writing.

References

Anderson, R.C., & Pearson, P.D. (1984). A schema-theoretic view of basic processes in reading comprehension. In P.D. Pearson (Ed.), *Handbook of reading research* (pp. 259–292). White Plains, NY: Longman.

Annis, L.F. (1985). Student-generated paragraph summaries and the information processing theory of prose learning. *Journal of Experimental Education, 54,* 4–10 .

Boyle, O.F., & Peregoy, S.F. (1990). Literacy scaffolds: Strategies for first- and second-language readers and writers. *The Reading Teacher, 44,* 194–200.

Bromley, K.D. (1991). *Webbing with literature: Creating story maps with children's books.* Needham Heights, MA: Allyn & Bacon.

Brown, H.D. (1980). *Principles of language learning and teaching.* Englewood Cliffs, NJ: Prentice Hall.

Bruner, J.S. (1978). The role of dialogue in language acquisition. In A. Sinclair, R. Jarvella, & W.J.M. Levant (Eds.), *The child's conception of language* (pp. 241–256). New York: Springer-Verlag.

Carrell, P.L. (1988). Some causes of text-boundedness and schema interference in ESL reading. In P.L. Carrell, J. Devine, & D.E. Eskey (Eds.), *Interactive approaches to second language reading* (pp. 101–113). New York: Cambridge University Press.

Carson, J.E., Carrell, P.L., Silberstein, S., Kroll, B., & Kuehn, P.A. (1990). Reading-writing relationships in first and second language. *TESOL Quarterly, 24,* 245–266.

Carson, J.E. (1990). Reading-writing connections: Toward a description for second language learners. In B. Kroll (Ed.), *Second language writing: Research insights for the classroom* (pp. 88–101). New York: Cambridge University Press.

Cullinan, B.E. (1989). *Literature and the child* (2nd ed.). San Diego, CA: Harcourt Brace.

Cummins, J. (1985). *The role of primary language development in promoting educational success for language minority students. In Schooling and language minority students: A theoretical framework.* Los Angeles, CA: California State University, Evaluation, Dissemination, and Assessment Center.

Cziko, G.A. (1978). Differences in first- and second-language reading: The use of syntactic, semantic, and discourse constraints. *Canadian Modern Language Review, 39,* 473–489.

Cziko, G.A. (1980). Language competence and reading strategies: A comparison of first- and second-language oral reading errors. *Language Learning, 30,* 101–116.

Dolly, M.R. (1990). Integrating ESL reading and writing through authentic discourse. *Journal of Reading, 33,* 360–365.

Dwyer, J. (1991). Talking in class. In J. Dwyer (Ed.), *A sea of talk.* Portsmouth, NH: Heinemann.

Dyson, A.H. (1984). Learning to write/learning to do school: Emergent writers' interpretations of school literacy tasks. *Research in the Teaching of English, 18,* 233–264.

Dyson, A.H., & Freedman, S.W. (1991) Writing. In J. Flood, J.M. Jensen, D. Lapp, & J.R. Squire (Eds.), *Handbook of research on teaching the English language arts.* New York: Macmillan.

Eckhoff, B. (1983). How reading affects children's writing. *Language Arts, 60,* 607–626.

Edelsky, C. (1982). Writing in a bilingual program. *TESOL Quarterly, 16,* 211–228.

Edelsky, C., Altwerger, B., & Flores, B. (1991). *Whole language: What's the difference?* Portsmouth, NH: Heinemann.

Faltis, C. (1993). *Joinfostering: Adapting teaching strategies for the multilingual classroom.* New York: Macmillan.

Ferreiro, E. (1990). Literacy development: Psychogenesis. In Y.M. Goodman (Ed.), *How children construct literacy: Piagetian perspectives.* (pp. 12–25). Newark, DE: International Reading Association.

Flood, J., & Lapp, D. (1988). Conceptual mapping strategies for understanding information texts. *The Reading Teacher, 41,* 780–783.

Flood, J., & Lapp, D. (1991). Reading comprehension instruction. In J. Flood, J.M. Jensen, D. Lapp, & J.R. Squire (Eds.), *Handbook of research on teaching the English language arts.* New York: Macmillan.

Grabe, W. (1991). Current developments in second language reading. *TESOL Quarterly, 25,* 375–406.

Hill, M. (1991). Writing summaries promotes thinking and learning across the curriculum—but why are they so difficult to write? *Journal of Reading, 34,* 536–539.

Kawakami-Arakaki, A.J., Oshiro, M.E., & Farran, D.C. (1989). Research to practice: Integrating reading and writing in a kindergarten curriculum. In J.M. Mason (Ed.), *Reading and writing connections.* Needham Heights, MA: Allyn & Bacon.

Kintsch, W., & van Dijk, T.A. (1978). Toward a model of text comprehension and production. *Psychological Review, 85,* 363–394.

Krapels, A. (1990). An overview of second language writing process research. In B. Kroll (Ed.), *Second language writing: Research insights for the classroom,* (pp. 37–56). New York: Cambridge University Press.

Krashen, S. (1981). The case for narrow reading. *TESOL Newsletter, 15,* 23.

Krashen, S. (1985). Bilingual education and second language acquisition theory. In *Schooling and language minority students: A theoretical framework.* Los Angeles, CA: California State University, Evaluation, Dissemination, and Assessment Center.

Kreeft, J.P., & Shuy, R.W. (1985). *Dialogue writing: Analysis of student-teacher interactive writing in the learning of English as a second language* (Final Report to the National Institute of Education, NIE-G-83-0030). Washington, DC: Center for Applied Linguistics.

Law, B., & Eckes, M. (1990). *More than just surviving: ESL for every classroom teacher.* Winnipeg, Man.: Peguis.

Mason, J.M. (Ed.). (1989). *Reading and writing connections.* Needham Heights, MA: Allyn & Bacon.

Peregoy, S., & Boyle, O. (1993). *Reading, writing, and learning in ESL: A resource book for teachers.* White Plains, NY: Longman.

Piper, T. (1993). *Language for all our children.* New York: Macmillan.

Pritchard, R. (1990). The effects of cultural schemata in reading processing strategies. *Reading Research Quarterly, 25,* 273–295.

Rigg, P., & Allen, V.A. (Eds.). (1989). *When they don't all speak English: Integrating the ESL student into the regular classroom.* Urbana, IL: National Council of Teachers of English.

Rosenblatt, L.M. (1985). Viewpoints: Transaction versus interaction—A terminological rescue operation. *Research in the Teaching of English, 19,* 96–107.

Rosenblatt, L.M. (1989). Writing and reading: The transactional theory. In J.M. Mason (Ed.), *Reading and writing connections* (pp. 153–176). Needham Heights, MA: Allyn & Bacon.

Salisbury, R. (1934). A study of the transfer effects of training in logical organization. *Journal of Educational Research, 38,* 241–254 .

Shanahan, T. (Ed.). (1990). *Reading and writing together: New perspectives for the classroom.* Norwood, MA: Christopher Gordon.

Smith, F. (1983). Reading like a writer. *Language Arts, 60,* 558–567.

Smith, F. (1992). Learning to read: The never-ending debate. *Phi Delta Kappan, 73,* 432–441.

Squire, J. (1983). Composing and comprehending: Two sides of the same basic process. *Language Arts, 60,* 581–589.

Staton, J., Shuy, R., Kreeft, J.P., & Reed, L. (1988). *Dialogue journal communication: Classroom linguistic social and cognitive views.* Norwood, NJ: Ablex.

Stotsky, S. (1983). Research on reading/writing relationships: A synthesis and suggested directions. *Language Arts, 60,* 627–642.

Thonis, E. (1989). Bilingual students: Reading and learning. In D. Lapp, J. Flood, & N. Farnan (Eds.), *Content area reading and learning: Instructional strategies* (pp. 105–113). Englewood Cliffs, NJ: Prentice Hall.

Urzua, C. (1987). "You stopped too soon": Second language children composing and revising. *TESOL Quarterly, 21,* 279–304.

Children's Books to Use in the ESL Classroom

Aardema, V. (1975). *Why mosquitoes buzz in people's ears: A West African tale.* New York: Dial.

Babbitt, N. (1975). *Tuck everlasting.* New York: Farrar, Straus & Giroux.

Bodecker, N.M. (1973). *It's raining, said John Twaining.* New York: Atheneum.

Demi. (1986). *Dragon kites and dragonflies.* San Diego, CA: Harcourt Brace.

Griego, M.C., Bucks, B.L., Gilbert, S.S., & Kimball, L.H. (1981). *Tortillitas para mama and other Spanish nursery rhymes.* New York: Holt, Rinehart.

Kalan, R. (1981). *Jump, frog, jump!* New York: Greenwillow.

Kraus, R. (1986). *Whose mouse are you?.* New York: Macmillan.

Martin, B., Jr. (1983). *Brown bear, brown bear, what do you see?* New York: Holt.

Reed, D.C. (1986). *Sevengill: The shark and me.* New York: Knopf.

Sattler, H.R. (1986). *Sharks, the super fish.* New York: Lothrop, Lee & Shepard.

Scieszka, J. (1989). *The true story of the 3 little pigs.* New York: Viking.

Wildsmith, B. (1982). *Cat on the mat.* New York: Oxford University Press.

Wolff, A. (1985). *Only the cat saw.* New York: Dodd Mead.

Wyndham, R. (1968). *Chinese Mother Goose rhymes.* New York: Philomel.

Alfredo Schifini

8

Language, Literacy, and Content Instruction: Strategies for Teachers

This chapter focuses on promoting academic achievement for second-language learners by facilitating comprehension of expository text. The presentation of instructional strategies centers on students in the upper-elementary grades. The discussion of reading in the content areas here is framed in the broader context of providing a comprehensive program for second-language speakers of English. In the upper grades, the academic demands and the demands of constructing meaning from text material make issues of language, literacy, and access to the core curriculum particularly acute. (See Cummins's discussion of cognitively demanding, context-reduced domains in chapter 3.) Although particulars of implementation vary, the program designs suggested focus on facilitating literacy and conceptual development for language-minority students.

The goals of this chapter are (1) to increase understanding among teachers at all levels of the multiple issues that have an impact on reading comprehension in the content areas for second-language speakers of English, (2) to provide greater insight into the development of comprehensive instructional programs for language-minority students, and (3) to suggest teaching strategies that both foster literacy development and facilitate conceptual growth through meaningful reading experiences.

Meeting the Language and Literacy Needs of Second-Language Learners

Developing an Instructional Program

As is pointed out throughout this volume, ESL students vary profoundly. Vast differences exist in their level of prior schooling and the opportunities they have had to develop high-level language and literacy in the home language. Students also differ greatly in terms of family background variables such as socioeconomic status, conditions under which they emigrated, degree of contact with the home country, and parents' expectations for their child's academic achievements (Ovando & Collier, 1985). Affective variables such as attitudes toward the acquisition of English, acculturation, and assimilation also play a role in creating diversity among students.

It is helpful for teachers at all levels to obtain as much cultural, linguistic, and factual information as possible about the diverse student populations that they serve. Caution must be exercised, however, to ensure that students' background profiles do not turn into a negative self-fulfilling prophecy. For example, we should not approach students from disadvantaged socioeconomic backgrounds who have had little education in their native countries with the assumption that it will be difficult or impossible for them to learn. Focusing on background factors that we do not control must not be used to channel less advantaged second-language learners into situations that do not maximize their potential (Ogbu & Matute-Bianchi, 1986; Skutnabb-Kangas & Toukomaa, 1976).

Before teachers even begin to develop strategies for the best use of content texts, they should consider what instructional practices have been implemented previously or are currently being carried out with target students to build fluency with academic language and literacy and to foster conceptual development. What type of preparation facilitates comprehension of expository text? Programs designed to promote high levels of language development, cognitive development, and positive self-esteem for second-language learners have several features in common (Krashen & Biber, 1988). A brief discussion of the characteristics of such programs follows.

The role of students' primary language. Success in a second language in academic settings depends greatly on the language base and literacy skill acquired in the first language (Cummins, 1989; Thonis, 1981). Programs that enable students to acquire initial literacy in their primary language or to expand on literacy development already begun in the home country are often most effective. Students who have developed strong linguistic knowledge in their own language bring a broader range of skills and concepts about language to the task of acquiring English. In addition, when programs incorporate students' primary language, parents can assume a larger role in their children's education.

In first-language programs, consideration should be given to the following:

1. Is supplemental reading material available in the first language for students to use for research projects, recreational reading, and other independent reading?

2. Do students have the opportunity to apply their first-language literacy skills by reading in the content areas?

3. Are students being given the message that bilingualism is an asset, and that English is to be added to their existing language skills?

When large numbers of students speak the same native language, it is sound and feasible to provide concept instruction in that language. When this is not possible because of a lack of bilingual teachers, it is still advisable to provide some primary-language support in the content areas for newly arrived ESL students. This may take many forms: for example, teacher assistants and other paraprofessional help, peer or cross-age tutors, community volunteers, and print material in the students' native tongue.

Language and literacy development in English as a second language. For speakers of other languages who do not receive significant primary-language instruction in English-speaking schools, it is particularly important to provide a print-rich language-development program in English. Children who enter the system without already-developed literacy, or those who will be dealing with print for the first time in English must be placed in contexts where they can comfortably construct meaning from print and use print to express themselves in meaningful ways. English-development activities should be student-centered and built on the learners' interests, curiosity, and strengths. Teachers should consider the following questions when designing their programs:

1. Are second-language learners who are new to English given the opportunity to perform many language tasks involving real or realistic communication?

2. Do they receive understandable language and multisensory input throughout the day?

3. Do they engage in reading and writing for authentic purposes daily?

4. Are the reading selections at the appropriate level of complexity, based on the students' evolving language and literacy skills in English?

5. Are second-language learners encouraged to take risks with language?

6. Are they integrated with native-English speakers in meaningful contexts?

7. Do they have access to challenging subject matter material and expository text delivered with a language-sensitive approach?
8. Is their growth in language arts assessed in an authentic fashion?

Preparing to Work with Expository Text

Focusing. If you are a classroom teacher with no specialized training in linguistics, how do you present content texts to students who have varied language and literacy backgrounds? Start by asking yourself some straightforward questions: How does any youngster come to comprehend and glean new information from text? Why are some students better with text material than others? What has worked well for students I have taught in the past?

Make a list of the successful strategies you have used in your teaching career. Just as students who are acquiring English are adding English to an existing language base, teachers can build on their repertoire of successful instructional approaches. Consideration must then be given to modifying these techniques to accommodate the wide range of second-language proficiency among the students. The focus will then be on what the students can do in terms of language tasks, and what the instructor can do to make the messages understandable.

Analyzing the text. Content text should be used purposefully for conceptual development. It is important for all students to be exposed to a variety of educational experiences designed to connect facts and concepts as well as to broaden understanding of text constructs. Expository text must not be approached as something to "cover" in the course of a semester or academic year, but rather as one of the many tools used by the students to uncover new ideas, concepts, and information. When teachers begin to rethink the role of text, many instructional strategies suggest themselves that are helpful in facilitating access to the content for second-language learners. Although these strategies have also proven to be effective with native-English speakers, their emphasis on concept development makes them particularly useful for ESL students. In preliminary planning teachers may find it useful to incorporate one or all of the following steps:

1. *Text structure.* Peruse the unit and note the overall structure or organization of the piece. Expository works, unlike narrative text, often do not use a story grammar or story structure that includes easily recognizable elements such as setting, characterization, problem, episodes, and resolution. Expository text tends to be complex and explanatory in nature. Common expository text structures include comparison-contrast, description, enumeration, sequencing, cause and effect, and problem-solution.

2. *Themes.* List as many themes as possible in the unit, chapter, or section of text to be read. Themes that are used across disciplines for in-depth analysis of a concept or topic will be easy for students to comprehend and relate to. Avoid theme studies that are historically or geographically limiting. Focus on broader themes that can be divided into subtopics, rather than on those that are subject specific. A topical theme such as dinosaurs is less desirable than one like patterns of change.

3. *Key concepts and main ideas.* Revisit the work to determine key concepts and main ideas. Rely on your own subject expertise or the school's curriculum guide or course of study. Look through the summary, chapter questions, and teacher's guide to refine choices. Keep in mind that many texts contain "professional detail," that is, facts that teachers of the subject find interesting. If these facts are simply presented to students to be memorized without connection to concepts or referents that are meaningful to them, the information will not be retained for long. Begin to consider how second-language learners can attain and use the concepts best, which is not necessarily the way the concepts were presented to you when you were a learner.

4. *Vocabulary.* Note vocabulary items that are absolutely indispensable for students to comprehend in order to grasp the concepts. In addition, list the vocabulary

with which second-language learners may have difficulty—for example, figures of speech or idiomatic expressions. Think of ways to relate the learning of key vocabulary to the constructs to be presented. Note ideas for vocabulary building that are interactive and can be related to the students' world.

5. *Text features.* Look through the section with attention to its features—visuals, timelines, maps, charts, graphs, subheads, bold print, italics, end of chapter summaries, and so on. Note any visual or graphic aspects that are particularly useful in facilitating understanding of the key ideas and concepts.

Assisting Students to Comprehend Content Material

Tapping, focusing, and building on students' background knowledge. The reading process, simply stated, is one in which the reader brings his linguistic and world knowledge to print to construct meaning. A key component for all readers is prior knowledge or schemata. Several studies of second-language speakers and reading comprehension indicate that prior cultural experiences are extremely important in comprehending text (Johnson, 1982; Steffensen, Joag-Dev, & Anderson, 1979). In some cases cultural origin of text plays a greater role in comprehension than does language complexity (Johnson, 1981). Teachers should tap and focus the prior knowledge of all their students. *Building* background, or inducing schemata, is particularly important for non-native speakers of English, especially those who have very low levels of English proficiency (Hudson, 1982).

In general, successful background-building activities involve one or more of the five senses; integrate listening, speaking, reading, and writing; and are motivating. Begin with simple, straightforward activities that are easy to carry out. The following suggestions for prereading activities related to students' background knowledge will be helpful:

1. *Visuals.* Have students work in small groups to make observations about visual stimuli, either those taken

from the text or ones that you supply. Help learners describe the visuals, speculate or hypothesize about them, and relate them to their own world. Include a variety of writing experiences in conjunction with the visuals. For example, students can record their observations, predictions, or inferences related to a primary-source document depicted in a social studies text and then share their written interpretations in a small-group or whole-class setting. Each member of a small group can contribute a response to make a group product. For example, in science class, the teacher might show a picture of waves breaking on a beach and ask how ocean water moves. Each student in the group writes an idea and passes the paper to the next person. After a brief period, the teacher highlights the most frequent responses and uses the students' interpretations of the pictures as an introduction to the text itself.

Obtaining visuals to use for prereading need not be an arduous task. Many textbooks present concepts in a cumulative form from grade to grade. Therefore, many fine visuals related to a main idea or concept may exist in texts at a lower grade level. In addition, students can be given an assignment to collect pictures related to a theme to be studied. Finally, commercial study prints are readily available. Whatever their source, visuals may be used to spur discussion and build background.

2. *Manipulatives and multimedia presentations.* Real objects and moving images make an instant impact on all learners. They are extremely useful in transcending language and building conceptual background. Concrete objects such as historical artifacts, posters, replicas of newspaper coverage of major historical events, and laboratory experiences with everyday objects such as thermometers, rocks, leaves, batteries, and bulbs all build background through interaction. Filmstrips, films, video and audio recordings, and some computer programs are extremely helpful as well as motivating.

These media should be used to build background knowledge across disciplines whenever possible. For example, during preparation to study a period of history in social studies class, prereading activities need not be limited to what students know about the political, social, and economic arrangements of the time but may include the building of additional schema with regard to religious beliefs, art and architecture, literature, law, technology, and the natural sciences. Students can work collaboratively to share as many features of a society as they can.

3. *Sharing prior experiences with students from diverse backgrounds.* Poems, musical selections, read-alouds of literature, diary entries, and newspaper and magazine articles all provide an opportunity for students to share their prior knowledge by their diverse responses to them. Interpretation should be related to prior knowledge through questioning and tied to predicting what will be read in the text. For example, after listening to the songs "We Shall Overcome" and "De Colores", students can share their personal experiences of or things they have in common related to discrimination and prejudice. Teachers might focus the discussion by asking questions such as these: "Why do you think people discriminate against other people? Have you ever felt discriminated against? How did you feel when you thought people were discriminating against you? Do you think we can change the way people think and help end discrimination? How have we tried to decrease discrimination in this country? The teacher may then ask students to predict what they might read about in a text on the Civil Rights movement in the United States. Students follow up by reading to confirm or refute their predictions or to refine ideas.

4. *Writing activities that focus students' prior knowledge.* Quick-writes, journal writing, and responding to writing prompts help in tapping background knowledge and building schemata. A quick-write is simply brainstorming in written form (see chapter 7). Teachers might instruct students to write for one minute about a given topic in a stream-of-consciousness form, without lifting the pen from the paper. Attention is not paid to mechanics, but rather to

ideas. Quick-writes are most successful when students are given clear instructions and some ideas to activate prior knowledge. As a prereading activity for a chapter on immigration, for example, teachers might have students think about the time in their lives when they moved to a new country, town, school, or home by asking themselves questions such as these: How did I feel? Was it fun, exciting, scary ? Did I want to go back? Why? Why not? Students can share their quick-writes by reading them aloud or talking about them.

Journals assist students in bringing background to text because they allow for personal response. For example, in preparation for reading about the use of child laborers in the industrial revolution, students can make entries in a fictitional diary of a 12-year-old factory worker.

Prompts that trigger a variety of written responses are also helpful. Students may complete open-ended sentences such as the following, in which the final product could range from a simple sentence to more complex conventional writing:

- There is so much pollution in the world because

  _____.

- People make war because _____

  _____.

5. *Linking prior knowledge to new concepts and ideas.* K-W-L (Ogle, 1986), a strategy designed for group instruction, is a three-part teaching model that actively involves students in the thinking processes involved when reading expository text, K—which stands for "what I know"—activates prior knowledge and when used collaboratively by members of a group, often helps individuals clarify misconceptions. W—"what I want to find out"—helps students establish their own purposes for reading and guides the reading. L—"what I have learned and still need to learn"—serves as a monitor for learning. There are many variations of activities that can be used with each component. These will benefit all students, but especially the

Strategies for Teachers

second-language learner who, with this procedure, is given the opportunity to immediately relate class discussion and his or her own thinking to the content (text) and to extend ideas beyond the text. The activities also give all students a chance to contribute regardless of their level of language proficiency, since everyone knows something and has something they want to learn. K-W-L can be used, with some modifications, in all content areas with informational text and with all groups.

The following are examples of activities for each component of the model:

1. Prereading (K and W)
    - Teacher and students brainstorm and chart what they already know about a topic. Everything that is said is written down, so that inaccuracies can be clarified.
    - As a class, students discuss what they want to learn.
    - As a group or individually, students categorize the information that they expect to use from the brainstorming session.
    - Students write their own questions on a student worksheet, such as the one shown in Figure 1.

2. During reading (L)
    - Students link what they know with new information.
    - Students read to confirm or reject information from the brainstorming session.
    - Students note answers to the questions they posed on the student worksheet.
    - Students jot down any questions that emerge from the reading.

3. Post Reading (L)
    - Students write what they have learned on the worksheet.

Figure 1
K-W-L Strategy Sheet

K—what we know	W—what we want to find out	L—what we learned and still need to learn

Categories of information we expect to use

A.
B.
C.
D.
E.
F.
G.

Reprinted by permission from Ogle (1986).

- Students share in their writing in small-group or whole-class settings, to review the questions answered by the reading.
- Teacher has additional materials available for reference when the answers to questions cannot be found in the text.
- Teacher maps information learned.
- Teacher writes a summary of the article.

The use of K-W-L with informational text will be an invaluable tool to second-language learners to broaden their conceptual knowledge and integrate information.

Vocabulary development. Vocabulary building with second-language learners sometimes causes confusion. The vocabulary presented in textbooks, preselected for emphasis by the publisher, may or may not be relevant for second-language learners. Most subject matter texts are designed for native speakers of English; multiple meanings and idioms may cause difficulty for ESL students, but not for native speakers. In some instances, texts foster the teaching of vocabulary in isolation because they introduce one concept and a related set of words at a time, rather than as connected to or interrelated with other concepts and words.

Confusion also arises when vocabulary development precedes concept development. Vocabulary instruction is most effective when it is used to label experiences or the concepts or constructs that have grown out of experiences. Consequently, teachers should attempt to provide concrete learning experiences whenever possible. Hands-on activities such as simulations, role-plays, dramatizations, games, demonstrations, and discovery experiments all provide for conceptual growth and development. These approaches also foster language and vocabulary development, because they provide a meaningful social context for learners to construct meaning while interacting with words.

Semantic-based vocabulary-building strategies, use of background knowledge, and word learning in the context of subject matter text are appropriate for students coming to English from diverse backgrounds. These general approaches are suggested in preference to dictionary, glossary, and association methods. Vocabulary development for second-language learners should help students develop word *knowledge* rather than word *memorization.*

The following are examples of semantic-based and interactive vocabulary-building activities appropriate for use with ESL learners:

1. *Semantic feature analysis.* With semantic feature analysis, students examine similarities and differences among words in a given category. This permits students to relate new words to words they already know. The procedure is direct and simple:

- A topic is selected from the text, emerges from discussion, or is chosen by the teacher and students.

- Words related to the topic are brainstormed by the students or taken from the text.

- Students develop a list of features shared by some of the words. Categories of features are grouped and written across the top of a chart; the words are written down the left to form a multicolumn chart. An example is shown in Figure 2.

- Students individually, in pairs, or small groups place plus or minus signs in the grid to indicate whether an item has the feature indicated.

- New words and features are added as a result of the reading.

2. *Semantic mapping.* Semantic mapping is an excellent tool for relating new ideas to learners' prior knowledge; it may also be used effectively as a vocabulary-building tool (see chapter 7's discussion of maps and webs). Through discussion, students relate terminology to concepts and organize them in a hierarchy, which is depicted visually in a map. When a reader sees a word from the

Figure 2
Semantic Feature Analysis of Shapes

	Four sided	Curved or rounded	Line segment	All sides equal in length	Right angles
Triangle	−	−	+	+	+
Rectangle	+	−	+	−	+
Parallelogram	+	−	+	+	+
Circle	−	+	−	−	−
Trapezoid	+	−	+	−	−
Semicircle	−	+	+	−	−
Square	+	−	+	+	+

Reprinted by permission from Stieglitz and Stieglitz (1981).

map in print, the map in its entirety will come to mind. Students should be encouraged to talk about the meaning of new words, new meanings for old words, and relationships among words. When vocabulary is taught in this fashion, it is more easily retained in memory.

The semantic map for musical instruments shown in Figure 3 (McNeil, 1992) illustrates how vocabulary is related at different levels of abstraction. The graphic shows that musical instruments have various properties, such as pitch and tone. Instruments are also related to other schemata. For example, the word *piano* may bring to the reader's mind more background knowledge concerning features of the instrument—polished ebony, 88 keys, grand versus upright, famous piano players, and so on. In this way, semantic maps can be extended to include a broad range of vocabulary and related concepts. //

3. *Interacting with vocabulary in context.* In vocabulary learning, context can be defined, in the narrowest sense, as the sentence or group of sentences in which the vocabulary is found. Gipe (1979) posits that if a learner relates a new word to an already existing schema, the word

Figure 3
A Semantic Map

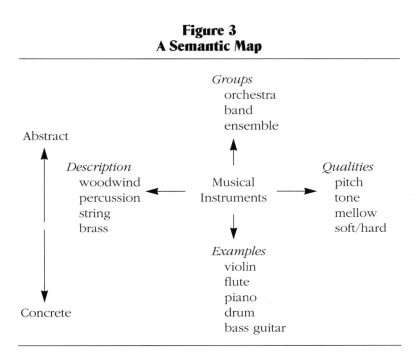

will be retained. Gipe's interactive vocabulary-learning method involves using the target word in three simple sentences, giving phrases that define the new item. This can be extended to give students practice in using the word. For example, a teacher could write the following statements on the board to help ESL students learn the word *despot*:

- The despot ruled his kingdom by terror, making all the citizens frightened of him.
- Despots are rulers who govern in a cruel way for their own benefit.
- Write down the names of any despots governing in the world today.
- Write as many things as you can think of that despots do to control their people.

Teaching the Structure of Expository Text

Organizational patterns. Direct teaching of the patterns that structure the presentation of new information in texts can greatly assist second-language learners in comprehending expository material (Armbruster, 1984). Teachers can begin by helping students recognize patterns in discourse such as cause and effect and comparison and contrast. Students then need to look for words that signal specific organizational patterns—for example, *therefore* and *because* for cause and effect, and *in contrast* and *compared to* for compare and contrast.

Here are some useful steps for teachers to follow in developing their students' awareness of discourse patterns:

1. Point out main patterns used by the author and words associated with that pattern.

2. Ask the students to look for examples of patterns and signal words in the text, and write them on chart paper.

3. Illustrate an example of the pattern on chart paper.

For example, a causation chart based on a reading about the Great Depression in the United States might list causes and effects in columns:

Cause	Effect
People bought stocks on margin.	When the stock market fell, they owed money on worthless investments.

When causal and temporal relationship are reflected in an organizational pattern in the text, an explanatory graphic organizer may help students with text comprehension. The teacher can supply the beginning of a graphic such as the one shown on the following page, and the students can collaborate to complete it:

Sometimes explanations might consist of several reasons for the same effect. For example, students may graphically represent the causes of World War I as below (Armbruster, 1985):

Nationalism

Militarism ⟶ World War I

Imperialism

To highlight compare and contrast patterns, teachers can guide students with certain questions and activities. For example, a teacher might ask students to read a passage on the Great Depression and compare and contrast its effects on rural dwellers, city dwellers, skilled workers, and unskilled workers.

Other patterns commonly found in expository text include enumeration, description, and sequencing (Meyer & Freedle, 1984). Enumeration involves presentation of a description or attributes so that the reader may relate them to key points and subtopics. Collection, like enumeration, involves grouping several descriptions or characteristics together. Sequencing in expository discourse usually involves the presentation of a major concept and then delineation of several steps of a process or events. The continued use of activities and guide to highlight all these structures will assist learners to use the text structure to relate information in the text to central ideas and construct meaning.

Outlining and relating information. Restructuring texts by outlining helps students synthesize, categorize, and highlight relationships. Most teachers are familiar with the traditional outline format. Information is organized in a hierarchy of ideas and concepts. The form utilizes Roman and Arabic numerals and upper- and lowercase letters to distinguish between categories, subcategories, and ideas.

Figure 4
An Array

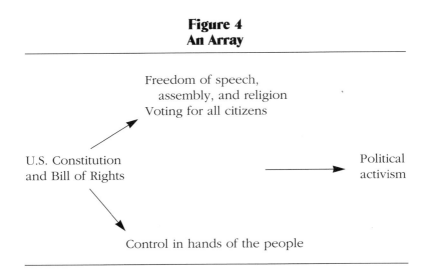

Freedom of speech,
assembly, and religion
Voting for all citizens

U.S. Constitution
and Bill of Rights

Political
activism

Control in hands of the people

Figure 5
A Radial

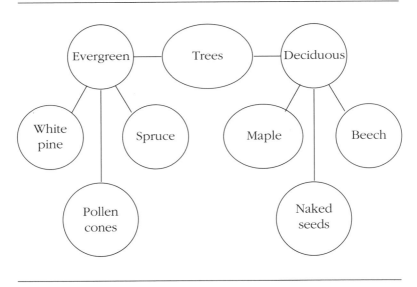

Evergreen

Trees

Deciduous

White
pine

Spruce

Maple

Beech

Pollen
cones

Naked
seeds

An alternative to linear outlining is the more free-form procedure called an array, an example of which is shown in Figure 4. The display of words depends on the creativity of the array's designer. Information from the text is taken into account, inferences are drawn, and key words or phrases are used to show supporting details, coordinate ideas or sequence. Figure 5 illustrates a radial, another free-form type of outline, that can be used to distinguish among coordinate, superordinate, and subordinate ideas. Although quite effective, radials tend to be less open-ended and therefore may limit inference and interpretation.

Teachers should also remember to teach ESL learners about the *wh* and *how* questions. When reading complex text it is often useful to pause and ask who, what, where, when, why, and how. Information gleaned from the text in relation to these questions can be represented in a *wh and how* graphic organizer.

Future Directions

Instructional approaches discussed in this chapter are quite straightforward. They build on students' strengths to enable them to interact with and construct meaning from print. Many of the strategies suggested are traditional. They reflect common-sense notions about how we come to know language and acquire literacy. Most content area teachers already use some of these approaches. As they encourage even more interaction and thereby set up new social contexts in their classrooms, a greater number of students will be able to engage in acts of real literacy—that is, in purposeful, meaningful reading and writing.

However, there is still much work to be done in ensuring students are able to construct meaning and acquire new information from content area texts. In broad terms, consideration must be given to the following if we are to sustain academic achievement, particularly for second-language learners: (1) research on various program designs that foster literacy and access to subject matter for linguistically and culturally diverse students, (2) research and teacher training in the area of authentic assessment of subject-matter mastery, (3) teacher training in the areas of first- and second-language and literacy development as well as reading in the content areas, (4) the development and utilization of a wide range of print and visual materials in conjunction with expository text, and (5) the development of multimedia materials tied to core curriculum in several of the main primary languages of our students.

Through the coordinated efforts of teachers, researchers, curriculum developers, policymakers, and community members, the goals of high levels of literacy and conceptual development for culturally and linguistically diverse student populations can be achieved.

References

Armbruster, B.B. (1984). The problem of "inconsiderate text." In G.G. Duffy, L.R. Roehler, & J. Mason (Eds.), *Comprehension instruction: Perspective and suggestions* (pp. 202–217). White Plains, NY: Longman.

Armbruster, B.B. (1985). Using graphic organizers in social studies. In *Ginn Occasional Paper #22*. Needham Heights, MA: Ginn.

Cummins, J. (1989). *Empowering minority students*. Sacramento, CA: California Association for Bilingual Education.

Gipe, J.P. (1979). Investigating techniques for teaching word meanings. *Reading Research Quarterly, 14*(4), 624–644.

Hudson, T. (1982). The effects of induced schemata on the short circuit in L² reading: Non-decoding factors in L² reading performance. *Language Learning, 32*, 1–31.

Johnson, P. (1981). Effects on reading comprehension of language complexity and cultural background of a text. *TESOL Quarterly, 15*, 169–181.

Johnson, P. (1982). Effects on reading comprehension of building background knowledge. *TESOL Quarterly, 16*, 503-516.

Krashen, S., & Biber, D. (1988). *On course: Bilingual education's success in California*. Sacramento, CA: California Association for Bilingual Education.

McNeil, J.D. (1992). *Reading comprehension: New directions for classroom practice*, 3rd. ed. New York: HarperCollins.

Meyer, B.J.F., & Freedle, R.O. (1984). Effects of discourse type on recall. *American Educational Research Journal, 2*(1), 121–143.

Ogbu, J.U., & Matute-Bianchi, M.E. (1986). Understanding socio-cultural factors: Knowledge, identity and school adjustment. In *Beyond language: Social and cultural factors in schooling language minority students* (pp. 73–142). Los Angeles, CA: Evaluation, Dissemination and Assessment Center, California State University.

Ogle, D. (1986). K-W-L: A teaching model that develops active reading of expository text. *The Reading Teacher, 39*(6), 164–170.

Ovando, C.J., & Collier, V.P. (1985). *Bilingual and ESL classrooms: Teaching in multicultural contexts.* New York: McGraw-Hill.

Skutnabb-Kangas, T., & Toukomaa, P. (1976). *Teaching migrant children's mother tongue and learning the language of the host country in the context of the sociocultural situation of the migrant family.* Helsinki: Finnish National Commission for the United Nations Educational, Scientific and Cultural Organization.

Steffensen, M., Joag-Dev, C., & Anderson, R.C. (1979). A cross-cultural perspective on reading comprehension. *Reading Research Quarterly, 15*, 10–29.

Stieglitz, E.L., & Stieglitz, V.S. (1981, October). Savor the word to reinforce vocabulary in the content areas. *Journal of Reading, 25*, 48.

Thonis, E.W. (1981). Reading instruction for language minority students. In *Schooling and language minority students: A theoretical framework* (pp. 147–181). Los Angeles, CA: Evaluation, Dissemination and Assessment Center, California State University.

Georgia Earnest García

9

Assessing the Literacy Development of Second-Language Students: A Focus on Authentic Assessment

ecently, in an attempt to improve students' academic performance, politicians and business leaders called for the expanded use of national tests in the United States (Rothman, 1991). The assumption behind these calls is that national tests will encourage teachers to better prepare their students to learn. Although these formal assessment measures might provide legislators and the general public with test scores that can be compared across states, it is extremely doubtful that they would lead to significant improvement in the literacy performance of language-minority students. In fact, for a variety of reasons, it is highly probable that second-language learners as a group would continue to score lower on such formal tests than their monolingual peers (Durán, 1983; García, 1991).

Formal test scores are difficult to interpret. Formal reading tests seldom provide information about *why* a student scores poorly. For instance, standardized reading-test scores do not differentiate among students' use of prior knowledge, reading strategies, or reasoning (Johnston, 1984; Royer & Cunningham, 1981). As a result, it is difficult to know whether students (monolingual and second language) do not perform well on a particular test because they do not know enough about the test's topics, cannot read the passages, or are unable to determine the "best" answers. Formal reading tests in English also fail to reflect the diverse cultural and language knowledge of children who are learning English as a second language. Research with Hispanic students (García, 1991) suggests that the English-reading-test performance of second-language speakers of English, as compared to that of monolingual English speakers, is more adversely affected by the range of passage topics included on the tests, the tendency of test writers to paraphrase key information from the text in the test questions, and the limited amount of time given to the students to complete the test. Another problem, and perhaps a more serious one for classroom decision making, is that reading-test scores do not indicate what monolingual or second-language students can and cannot do on "authentic" literacy tasks, tasks that mirror the way literacy is used in "real life" (for a more complete discussion, see García and Pearson, 1991b).

Simply put, test scores do not provide enough information to help teachers plan their instruction effectively. To plan instruction, teachers need to know how students are approaching, interpreting, and engaging in authentic literacy tasks. Teachers working with second-language students also need to know how these students are using their two languages to make sense of the literacy tasks before them. It is the thesis of this chapter that authentic assessment, sometimes termed informal or situated assessment, can provide a more comprehensive profile of the second-language learner's literacy strengths and weaknesses than can more formal assessment measures.

The chapter begins with a brief review of the different types of formal assessment measures that have been used to evaluate the language and literacy performance of second-language students. Then the merits of authentic assessment are discussed, and various types of classroom activities that teachers can use to evaluate and facilitate the literacy development of second-language students are described. The chapter concludes with some final thoughts about the literacy assessment of second-language students.

Formal Assessment Measures

Many children encounter formal tests even before they actually attend school. For example, before she starts kindergarten, Marta, a child from a Spanish-speaking background, will probably be given a language-proficiency test to evaluate her oral-language proficiency in English and to determine whether she should be placed in a Spanish or English kindergarten. If she is placed in an English classroom, then in all likelihood she will be confronted with the same types of formal tests that native-English-speaking students face, even if her English is not as proficient as is her peers'. For example, her teacher might give her a reading readiness test in English. When she is older, she will periodically take standardized reading-achievement tests. If she is in a school district that uses a basal reading program, then she will complete the tests provided in the program. If Marta lives in one of the 41 U.S. states that have developed their own statewide reading-achievement tests, then she will take this test at some point while she is in school.

Marta's experiences with formal tests will not be much different if she is placed in a bilingual or English as a second language program funded by the state or federal government. Throughout the program, she will periodically take English-language-proficiency tests and standardized reading-achievement tests in English to determine if she is capable of leaving the second-language program for the English classroom.

What do any of these tests tell the teacher about Marta's literacy performance? García and Pearson (1991b) caution that formal tests are, at best, *samples of performance*. What they sample clearly depends on their purpose and theoretical framework. How well they sample second-language children's literacy knowledge depends on the extent to which they reflect the children's literacy development, varied levels of bilingualism, and diverse vocabulary and background knowledge.

The next section of this chapter takes a closer look at the types of tests that might be given to Marta. These include language-proficiency tests, reading readiness tests, standardized reading-achievement tests, basal tests, and statewide reading tests. (Much of the discussion on standardized, basal, and statewide reading tests is based on García and Pearson, 1991b.)

Language-Proficiency Tests

Language-proficiency measures generally sample students' knowledge of a particular language. Together with other measures, they are frequently used to determine which of a bilingual child's languages is dominant or to determine when second-language learners are ready to perform in an all-English classroom. The tests tend to measure language skills that the test developers consider essential to language fluency. These include phonology (the pronunciation and identification of sounds), morphology (knowledge of inflectional suffixes or word endings), syntax (grammatical structure of sentences), and lexicon (vocabulary). Obviously, the extent to which language-proficiency-test scores measure the language competence of individual students depends on the degree to which the composite skills on the test reflect students' actual language knowledge and language experiences.

Savignon (1983) argues that it is possible for students to score well on these tests based on their grammatical competence in the language without knowing how to use the language in real-life situations. For example, students may score well on a test but not understand teachers' instructions to perform particular tasks nor comprehend their explanations about new concepts.

Cummins (1981, 1984) and Troike (1982) warn educators against overreliance on language-proficiency-test scores to determine when students know enough English to perform in an English classroom. Their concern is based on the fact that the tests emphasize linguistic aspects of second-language children's speaking and listening development in English but provide very little information about their reading and writing development. Cummins (see chapter 2) reports that based on their oral proficiency in English, many second-language children are placed prematurely in all-English classrooms without first developing the literacy needed in their native language and in English to achieve academically. Although these children may appear to communicate well in spoken English, many of them do not have the literacy necessary to learn information from text.

A further limitation of the tests is that they do not reflect second-language children's bilingualism. For instance, second-language children at the preschool and kindergarten levels may be acquiring English and their native language in different settings. As a result, some of these children may know some vocabulary concepts in one language but not in the other. Because language-proficiency measures only evaluate children's knowledge of one language at a time, they underestimate children's total knowledge.

Reading Readiness Tests

Reading readiness tests typically include subtests of letter recognition, shape perceptions, sound-symbol correspondences, and oral vocabulary. Stallman and Pearson (1990) point out that the readiness concept underlying these tests contradicts the notion of children's developmental or emerging knowledge about literacy. It implies that children must go through discrete stages before they can engage successfully in beginning literacy tasks.

Some reading readiness tests have been criticized for cultural bias because they use vocabulary and pictures representative of middle-class, native-English-speakers' experiences (Hall, Nagy, & Linn, 1984). In addition, many of the English versions assess prereading potential based on children's pronunciation of standard English. If children are not orally fluent in English, obviously they will not score well on the English version of the test even if they can accomplish many of the tasks measured by it.

Another problem with the tests is that they do not reveal what bilingual children already know about reading and writing in one language that could be transferred to reading and writing in another language. For example, children who know the letter names in their native language probably will have an easier time learning letter names in their second language. Similarly, there is considerable evidence that children who already understand the function of reading in their native language have less difficulty learning to read in a second language than do children without this awareness (Downing, 1984; Modiano, 1973).

Standardized Reading-Achievement Tests

Although many educators have warned against overreliance on standardized reading-achievement-test scores for placement and instructional purposes, they are still used for these purposes (García, 1991). Educators frequently use the test scores to track or group students "homogeneously," assuming that by doing so, they are meeting students' individual needs (García, Pearson, & Jimenez, 1990). The test scores reported are usually norm-referenced—that is, the score indicates the performance of individual students relative to that of other students who have taken similar versions of the test.

Standardized reading tests have been criticized because their format and content do not reflect current reading theory (Edelsky & Harman, 1988). Valencia and Pearson (1987) point out that students' test scores represent their performance on a variety of subskills related to reading (literal recall, vocabulary recognition, and main-idea identification) but provide little information about the reading strategies that students use or whether students know how and when to apply these strategies to new situations. Because the test passages are brief and frequently contrived, they lack the structural and topical integrity of authentic text. Moreover, the questions are not based on inferencing and text-structure taxonomies and tend to overemphasize students' literal comprehension. For second-language children, there are various additional concerns associated with standardized tests. Several researchers suggest that standardized tests may be less reliable and valid with second-language students than with monolingual students (Durán, 1983; García, 1988). The test developers do not acknowledge that second-language students may not be as familiar with the topics included on the tests as their English-speaking counterparts (García, 1988, 1991), nor do they take into account the students' emerging language proficiency in English. For example, I found that even fifth and sixth grade bilingual Hispanic students who had been enrolled in all-English classrooms for at least two years were misled by the presence of paraphrased vocabulary in standardized-reading-test items. When I translated a few of the key words paraphrased in the test questions into Spanish, some of the students' answers demonstrated that they had understood the passages even though their performance on the multiple-choice questions suggested otherwise. The latter finding is consistent with other research that has shown that bilingual students frequently produce more comprehensive recall of text written in their second language when they are permitted to use their first language (Eaton, 1980; Lee, 1986).

Other factors that adversely affect the reading-test performance of bilingual students as compared to that of monolingual students include the semantic content of key vocabulary and students' lack of familiarity with test-taking strategies. In addition most of the bilingual students I interviewed needed more time to complete the tests than did monolingual English-speaking students (García, 1991). This is an interesting finding given that "true" bilinguals generally take longer to process text in either language than monolinguals, especially texts in their second language (Chamot, 1980; Eaton, 1980; Mägiste, 1979).

Tests from Basal Reading Programs

Other reading-achievement tests frequently used in the classroom are those developed by publishers of basal reading programs. These tests are similar in format to standardized reading tests except that they tend to reflect the curriculum covered in the basal reading series. They are also criterion-referenced: that is, they do not compare one student's performance to that of others, but instead compare it to a predetermined standard to see if it reflects a certain level of competence.

Clearly, the performance of second-language children on these tests is affected by many of the same factors that influence their performance on standardized reading tests. In addition, these tests assume that all students taking them have had the same opportunity to acquire the vocabulary, topical knowledge, and skills presented in the reading series. Although second-language students enrolled in all-English classrooms may progress through the series, the extent to which they acquire the same vocabulary, topical knowledge, and skills as their monolingual counterparts may differ considerably, depending on the type of instruction they have received, their prior knowledge, and their English fluency (García, 1988). Second-language students who have not used the series obviously will be at a disadvantage on the series test, as will students recently moved from a bilingual classroom to an all-English one. If the students' previous instructional program focused on authentic literacy tasks, they probably will be unfamiliar with the decontextualized tasks that are frequently used on the basal tests to sample students' reading and writing development (Foertsch & Pearson, 1987; García & Pearson, 1991b).

Statewide Reading Tests

Many statewide tests have been developed in an attempt to reflect current reading theory more accurately. For example, the state reading tests in Illinois and Michigan assess students' prior knowledge of reading passages; provide them with longer, uncontrived passages; ask questions tied to inferencing and text-structure taxonomies; and evaluate students' awareness of reading strategies and their attitude toward reading (Valencia & Pearson, 1987; Wixson et al., 1987). Clearly, these changes are major improvements in the large-scale testing of reading.

On the other hand, the tests are based on monolingual readers' experiences and, like standardized reading tests, do not take into account the unique factors that may affect second-language students' English-reading-test performance. Before the tests are heralded as better measures of second-language children's English reading, additional research is needed to examine the relation between these children's literacy development and their reading performance on the tests (García, 1991). A major problem with the statewide tests, as with all formal tests, is that second-language students frequently reveal greater comprehension of what they have read in their second language if they are allowed to use their first language (Chamot, 1980; García; Lee, 1986). This is a problem that test writers have not been able to resolve.

The Merits of Authentic Assessment

Authentic assessment usually refers to classroom-based assessment of students by teachers (Valencia, McGinley, & Pearson, 1990). Until recently, authentic assessment was not highly regarded by many researchers and educators because it did not result in "objective" measures of students' performance (García & Pearson, 1991b). Educators were interested in obtaining information that would allow them to compare student performance across sites. This meant that evaluative criteria needed to be used consistently with different student populations. Critics considered teacher evaluation of student performance to be subjective and unreliable, because teachers do not always articulate and consistently apply the criteria they use for evaluation. In the area of second-language learning, critics of authentic assessment pointed out that teachers did not always know the languages the children spoke, nor were they knowledgeable about first- and second-language acquisition and bilingualism (August & García, 1988).

New theories of literacy and learning have resulted in a shift in how authentic assessment is viewed. The purpose of assessment has widened to include teacher decision-making and provide information on what teachers need to know in order to make informed decisions about the literacy development of individual students in the classroom. This shift in perspective meshes with the constructivist view of reading (García & Pearson, 1991b). Educators and researchers are now very interested in understanding children's attitudes toward reading and their knowledge about reading. They want to know how students approach reading tasks, the types of reading strategies they use, and the different factors that influence their reading comprehension—aspects of the reading process that are not readily reflected in traditional assessment measures.

Authentic assessment procedures are developed by teachers and can be used both to evaluate and to facilitate children's academic performance and development. Unlike formal assessment measures that are almost always commercially produced and not necessarily an integral part of individual teachers' ongoing instructional plans, authentic assessment activities are part of the classroom environment. The activities do not take away from instructional time because they become part of instruction. These classroom-situated assessment techniques address the issue of authenticity that plagues many formal measures, because teachers can use them to evaluate how children approach and how well they accomplish authentic literacy tasks. The assessment also takes into account the classroom context and reflects individual students' progress and learning.

Authentic Assessment Activities

In deciding how to proceed with authentic assessment in the classroom, teachers of second-language learners can ask themselves two questions:

1. What do I need to know about individual children's literacy and language development in order to plan their instruction?
2. What activities and tasks can I use to find out and record this information?

The response to the first question requires teachers to reflect on the reading process and second-language children's literacy development. For example, in assessing any child's literacy development, it is helpful to know about his or her interests and attitudes toward reading and how he or she defines the reading task. It is also helpful to know the extent to which children can appropriately activate, maintain, and switch schemata; make appropriate inferences at the word, sentence, and text levels; vary their approach to text; monitor their comprehension; and use appropriate comprehension strategies and repair them when their comprehension goes awry (García & Pearson, 1991a). In terms of second-language children, it is helpful to know where these students are in their bilingual and biliterate development. Factors that may influence students' biliterate development include their attitudes toward reading in both languages, their bilingual reading experiences and expertise, and their language development in both languages.

The response to the second question requires teachers to evaluate the usefulness of the different literacy activities that currently constitute their classroom instruction. In planning an authentic assessment program, teachers need to decide which activities they will use to document certain aspects of their students' literacy development. Information gained from the activities should help teachers plan instruction as well as provide them with a basis for student evaluation.

There are a variety of authentic assessment techniques and measures that can be used in the classroom. Activities that may be particularly useful to teachers dealing with second-language students in the all-English or bilingual setting include classroom observations, oral-miscue analysis, story retellings, story tellings, tape-recording of oral reading, reading logs, reading response logs, think-alouds, writing folders, and student-teacher conferences.

Classroom observation. Teacher observation is frequently touted as a way to keep track of students' literacy development. However, as Geneshi cautions (1985), teachers are often too busy to note everything that happens to individual students in a classroom.

Anecdotal records and individual or group charts are two ways that teachers can begin systematically to document their students' literacy development. When teachers use anecdotal records (Bird, 1989; Geneshi, 1985), they record key observations as well as their interpretation of the events. They can do this by making notes on index cards, self-adhesive removable notes, address labels, or in loose-leaf binders or spiral notebooks. Anecdotal records usually involve spontaneous observations about children's actual behavior. For instance, a teacher may note that Min-Ling wrote her address in English for the first time, or that Ahmed had difficulty comprehending the volcano story because he did not appear to know what a volcano was. Once teachers have made the initial notes, they follow through with their observations by recording related events on subsequent days.

Another way teachers can record their observations is by using charts. Charts are quite similar to checklists (Dalrymple, 1989; Hood, 1989), except that space is available for comments and the categories or headings are more subject to change. In most cases, teachers will list on the chart certain categories that they are interested in observing. As they use the chart, they may modify or add to it to reflect more accurately their students' progress. For example, a kindergarten teacher may notice that while playing in a housekeeping center, Tuan initiates a conversation with a native-English-speaking child—something that the teacher has not observed before. The teacher can quickly note this under the heading "Use of Oral English," writing in the box "s.i. con. w/Joe" (student-initiated conversation with Joe).

Under the heading "Use of Written English," the teacher may record that Han wrote his own English caption for a story he illustrated with another child by writing "Eng. story cap." Charts can be placed on clipboards and located in strategic spots throughout the classroom so they are easily accessible. They can be used to document the progress of individual children or a group.

Different skills can be listed on the charts, taking into account students' grade levels, literacy development, and bilingualism. For instance, teachers can use charts to document the progress of second-language children in recognizing and using English. If teachers do not speak the children's native languages, they can ask parents, bilingual aides, or peers to tell them what the children know in the native language. If, for example, a child knows how to identify colors in the native language, the teacher may note when that child first demonstrates that she or he recognizes the English words for various colors by following oral or written instructions that use these words. The teacher might also record when the child first says the words, reads them, or includes them in a piece of writing. Another way to use charts is to note how individual children choose to read or write during free time, documenting the extent to which the children read and write in their native language or English. Teachers can also use the charts to record the extent to which individual students ask or answer different types of inferencing questions. They can note whether students are able to answer questions with or without the help of their teacher or peers.

Through classroom observation and the use of anecdotal records or charts, teachers can keep track of students' progress throughout the school year. Both monolingual and bilingual teachers can use these records to document when second-language children experience difficulties with English vocabulary concepts or syntax, what type of assistance is offered to help them resolve the difficulties, how the children respond, and when the item no longer presents difficulty. Used creatively, anecdotal records and charts can help provide a more complete picture of second-language children's emerging second-language proficiency and literacy development.

Oral-miscue analysis. Monolingual and bilingual teachers can also conduct oral-miscue analysis of students' oral reading to determine the different types of reading strategies the students employ. This requires some advance planning in that teachers need to have a transcript of the text to be read. As students read aloud, teachers note on the text any repetitions, substitutions, insertions, omissions, or self-corrections students make. Analysis of these data tells teachers the extent to which students are using graphophonic, syntactic, semantic, and discourse cue systems. (For a complete discussion of the technique, see Goodman, Watson, and Burke, 1987.) A more thorough analysis includes asking students to retell what was read (as in story retelling, discussed in the next section).

If monolingual teachers are not sure whether second-language students' miscues represent pronunciation or developmental errors, they should ask clarification questions to see whether students have understood what they read (García & Pearson, 1991b). If teachers are bilingual or if they have access to bilingual aides, it is helpful to conduct oral-miscue analyses of students' reading in both languages. This is one way to safeguard against being misled by second-language students' less-than-fluent oral English. Although second-language students may encounter difficulties with unfamiliar vocabulary or syntactic structures (especially structures that are peculiar to the second language), those who are literate in their native language can typically use their existing expertise to approach reading in their second language. If these students understand that the purpose of reading is to construct meaning, they will tend to make fewer uncorrected graphophonic miscues (not saying *horse* for *hose,* for example, when it is clear that *horse* does not make sense) than students who are not particularly literate in either language (Hudelson, 1981).

Story retelling. Teachers can also ask students to retell what they have read. Teachers have a story map in front of them, and quickly check off the points that students include as they retell (Morrow, 1989). A simple story map typically includes headings that focus on the story setting (time, place, and principal characters), the problem or goal, initiating event, plot events or episodes, and resolution (for examples of story maps, see Muth, 1989; Tierney, Readence, & Dishner, 1990). Obviously, some stories require complex story maps. After students have finished the retelling, teachers can ask probing questions to elicit additional information about the story that students may not have included. If students have varied from the story in the retelling, teachers can review the story with students in order to understand what precipitated the deviation. This procedure can provide teachers with useful information about where and how students' comprehension goes awry.

Teachers need to remember that many second-language students will give fuller accounts of what they read if they are allowed to use their first language when they do not know or cannot recall key vocabulary terms in English (García, 1991). If teachers are monolingual English speakers, they can tape-record students' retellings and then ask bilingual parents, aides, or tutors to listen with them to the tapes. Bilingual assistants can translate for teachers what students have said in their native languages, and together they can determine what students have understood.

Another option is to allow second-language students of varying English proficiency from the same language background to do story retellings in pairs. The students first read the story silently. Then the teacher gives one of them a completed story map. The other student retells the story while the first student listens, checking off the information on the story map. The two students then discuss the parts of the story that the reteller did not understand by referring back to the story and noting on the story map unknown terms, concepts, or syntactic structures. The students can then switch roles with a different story. This technique allows teachers to discover what students comprehend and provides valuable information about students' emerging English-language proficiency and biliterate status.

Story telling or writing. A useful way to assess children's developing literacy in English is to ask them to tell or write a story in response to a series of pictures or to a wordless picture book. Young children can tape-record their story telling, while older children can write their story. If teachers are working with second-language students and do not understand their native languages, they can encourage students to tell as much of the story as possible in English, filling in the gaps with their native languages. Then bilingual aides, tutors, parents, or other students can discuss the items in the native languages with individual students, later translating them into English for teachers.

Both oral and written story telling indicate to teachers what students have learned about the conventions of narrative English text. They also provide teachers with additional information about students' developing English-language proficiency. Perhaps most important, if bilingual aides are available, their dialogues with students and discussions with teachers can help identify those areas where students need additional help.

Tape-recordings of oral reading. Teachers can periodically have students tape-record their oral reading (Routman, 1988). Ideally, students should be given the option to choose the selection they want to read, to rehearse it, and, when ready, to tape-record their performance. Tapes of students' oral reading provide teachers with information about students' expressive reading and reading fluency. By reviewing the sets of tapes that students have recorded over the semester or year, teachers can also note the different types of readings that students choose to submit. If students are not choosing a variety of texts or if teachers want to determine whether students can read more difficult texts, teachers can also ask students to read designated texts.

If students are biliterate, teachers can suggest that students make tapes in both languages. Although teachers may not understand students' native languages, listening to students' oral readings in those languages and reviewing books that students read can give teachers some understanding about what level students feel capable of reading in their native languages. It also encourages students to read in both languages, helping to promote students' biliteracy and to validate the worthiness of students' home languages in a school context.

Reading logs. Students can also benefit by keeping an ongoing record of the different types of materials they are reading (Atwell, 1987; Routman, 1988). In a reading log, students record the author and title of the different stories and books they have read, noting the date they completed the text. Teachers review the logs periodically, noting the types of materials and genres that the students are reading as well as the number of books. Sometimes, teachers combine the reading log with a response log (see the next section). At other times, they ask the students to write a short annotation for each item read.

If teachers are working with students from diverse linguistic and cultural backgrounds, the students should be encouraged to expand the categories listed in the logs to include newspaper and magazine articles, letters, and other types of texts that might be common in some of the students' homes (Edwards & García, 1991). Second-language students should be asked to list what they are reading in both of their languages, at school and at home. This will encourage them to read both in and out of school.

Reading-response logs. Reading-response logs are notebooks in which students record their responses to what they read, and teachers reply to those responses (Atwell, 1987; Routman, 1988). Teachers who use reading-response logs generally encourage students to react personally to what they read. In a sense, response logs become dialogues between students and teachers about books the students are reading. Some students may find it difficult to react personally to a text and instead will simply summarize what they have been reading. Although summaries can be a useful assessment tool, they do not allow teachers and students to carry on a conversation. They can also be quite boring for teachers to read, especially when a number of students read and summarize the same book. So, while many teachers initially accept summaries, they generally try to "nudge" students to react to the story by asking them questions. For example, if a child is responding to a Frog and Toad story, the teacher may write, "Ruey-Chuan, if you were acting out the Frog and Toad story, which character would you want to be, Frog or Toad? Why?" or "It sounds as though you like Toad best. Can you tell me why?"

Teachers who use reading-response logs in their classrooms often collect them from students on a rotating basis. Teachers may respond in writing to students' entries or discuss them with students in conferences.

Response logs provide teachers with information about how students are synthesizing and interpreting information from their reading. They also allow teachers to see what students are reading and what they think is particularly noteworthy or important. Sometimes students will write about topics that they are hesitant to discuss in front of the class. In addition, teachers can use the logs to monitor and aid students' writing development. In short, both reading and writing performance can be enhanced and assessed with reading-response logs.

Through response logs, teachers can also observe students' biliterate development. If they encourage students to read and write in both languages, they can note the types of materials that students are reading in their two languages. If teachers are monolingual English speakers, they can ask bilingual students to work together or with English-speaking students to translate or write some of the responses in English. Over time, they can observe bilingual students' development in written English.

Think-alouds. Teachers can also ask students to engage in think-alouds (Tierney, Readence, & Dishner,

1990). Think-alouds work best when they have first been modeled by the teacher. For example, teachers can share how they are making sense of a text by orally or silently reading a text for a moment and then interrupting the reading to talk about their thought processes. A teacher might say, "The title suggests that this story will be about a craft fair. I'll read on to see. Oops, I don't know what this word 'fuliginous' means. Maybe if I read more, I can figure it out. Oh, I guess my original prediction wasn't correct. It's about an oven, not a craft fair."

The easiest type of think-aloud is prompted, where teachers have used their knowledge of narrative or expository text to mark the text with asterisks at key points. Students read the text, either aloud or silently, and stop reading when they reach the asterisk. At this point, teachers usually ask students to explain what they have read, to identify any problems that they have had in comprehending the text, and to say what they anticipate will happen in the next section. If students' explanations about what was read do not conform to what teachers expect, teachers may ask students, "How did you determine that?" or "Can you show me where you got that idea?"

In the process of using think-alouds, teachers can also help individual students monitor their reading. For example, if a student misinterprets a vocabulary term, the teacher can ask the student to reread several sentences where the term was used in context and then ask, "Based on these sentences, what do you think the term means?" Or, if a student is not self-monitoring, the teacher can ask, "Given what you've read, does what you said make sense?" The interactive nature of think-alouds and their emphasis on active construction of meaning send students the message that reading is a strategic activity that involves using what you know in concert with the text.

Think-alouds can be particularly informative when used with second-language students. Through this type of dialogue, teachers can discover not only the types of challenges that students encounter with the text, but also how they deal with such challenges. For example, a teacher might discover that Rafael relied on one meaning of a word when another meaning was called for, or that Shobha misinterpreted the text because she was not familiar with key vocabulary or activated inappropriate schemata. Once teachers are aware of these problems and how they affect students' engagement with the text, they can deal with the problems in their classroom instruction.

Think-alouds can also be used with small groups of students. In this case students can tape-record their interactions as they work together to complete a prompted think-aloud. In a subsequent session, teachers can review the tape with students, asking them to explain the challenges they faced and to what extent they resolved them. Again, teachers need to understand that second-language students may use both languages in the process of constructing meaning from the text.

Think-alouds require planning but can be used with students periodically throughout the school year. Dated tape-recordings of think-alouds provide teachers with an ongoing record of student progress.

Writing folders. Writing folders or portfolios include samples of students' written work collected over time (Atwell, 1987; Routman, 1988). Teachers should encourage students to keep their drafts, revisions, and final copies in the folders as well as works in progress (García & Pearson, 1991b). The folder can contain formal as well as informal pieces. The latter might include written activities that relate to students' reading and English-language development, such as story maps, graphic organizers or flow charts, notes for research papers, and students' own vocabulary lists or personal dictionaries. Even very young children can produce writing that, although unsophisticated, demonstrates their emerging literacy. For example, young children can title or describe their drawings as well as write their own stories by using invented spelling. Dating work and storing it in a portfolio allows teachers to keep a running record of children's progress.

Writing folders allow teachers to see a somewhat different aspect of bilingual students' language and literacy development because they can indicate the extent to which students are using their two languages to construct meaning. Bilingual students should be free to use both languages to plan and revise text and be encouraged to keep various versions of a text in their folders, although monolingual English-speaking teachers may want to see a final product in English.

If students do a lot of writing and teachers do not want to review it all, they can ask students to select what they consider to be their best work. Students can then give teachers the final product as well as the various drafts that went into its preparation. Teachers need to see how students progressed throughout the writing process if they are to further students' writing development. Having students select the pieces that will be evaluated gives them the opportunity to participate in their own evaluation. Teachers need to provide students with this opportunity if they want students to view reading and writing as communication and to monitor their own reading and writing.

Student-teacher conferences. Individual conferences between students and teachers provide an opportunity to set goals and discuss the students' progress (Atwell, 1987; Routman, 1988). Together, students and teachers can review some of the documents produced by the authentic assessment program. Teachers can ask students to explain how they approached and completed some of the key tasks. Personal conversations with students about their work give teachers the opportunity to find out more about students' attitudes toward and interest in reading. In addition, teachers can use the time to ask second-language students how they view their progress in the two languages. They can also ask students to identify what they are currently finding easy and difficult to do. This procedure may uncover unique problems or questions teachers never anticipated.

Some Final Thoughts

We need to understand why many second-language students do not score well on formal literacy measures in English. Formal literacy measures provide a sampling of student performance. Because formal literacy tests often underestimate the reading performance of second-language students (García, 1991), teachers of these students need to look beyond these tests to understand students' literacy performance. This does not mean that formal literacy measures cannot be used but that they need to be used cautiously and in concert with authentic assessment measures.

Teachers can learn more about how their students are approaching, interacting with, and responding to text when they incorporate authentic assessment activities into classroom instruction. One strength of authentic assessment activities is that they can become an integral part of the curriculum. Their incorporation into the curriculum can help facilitate students' comprehension while providing teachers with information about students' literacy development, interests, and attitudes.

Authentic assessment programs work best when teachers organize activities so that information about the students' literacy development is collected over time. This type of documentation is needed if teachers are to track student progress and use authentic assessment activities for evaluative or report-card purposes.

Teachers also need to use a variety of activities in assessment. One of the features of authentic assessment programs is that they provide multiple indexes of performance. In a sense, the multiple indexes offer teachers multiple lenses through which to view students. To use these to understand the literacy performance of second-language students, teachers need to find out as much as they can about students' literacy experiences in their first and second languages at home and at school. They especially need to widen "the range of explanations they consider as they try to understand why some students are not performing well in the classroom" (García & Pearson, 1991b, p. 270).

Teachers and administrators need to be open to input from students' parents or other community or school personnel who know the students' language and culture. Without this information and without a willingness to allow students to continue to use their two languages to construct meaning, teachers will replicate many of the problems inherent in using formal assessment measures.

Finally, authentic assessment relies on teachers' expertise. Teachers who are interested in authentic assessment need to be knowledgeable about the literacy process. Authentic assessment provides one means for teachers to find out the strengths and weaknesses of students' ongoing literacy development. However, teachers need to know how to interpret these data. This means that teachers take on additional responsibility. If they work with second-language children, they need to make a concerted effort to become knowledgeable about first- and second-language acquisition and literacy processes. Teachers also need to find out as much as they can about students' language use and culture. Without this knowledge, authentic assessment will be no more useful than formal assessment.

References

Atwell, N. (1987). *In the middle: Writing, reading, and learning with adolescents.* Portsmouth, NH: Heinemann.

August, D., & García, E.E. (1988). *Language minority education in the United States: Research, policy, and practice.* Springfield, IL: Charles C Thomas.

Bird, L.B. (1989). The art of teaching: Evaluation and revision. In K.S. Goodman, Y.M. Goodman, & W.J. Hood (Eds.), *The whole language evaluation book* (pp. 15–24). Portsmouth, NH: Heinemann.

Chamot, A.U. (1980, November). Recent research on second-language reading. *National Association of Bilingual Education (NABE) Forum*, 3–4.

Cummins, J. (1981). The role of primary language development in promoting educational success for language minority students. In *Schooling and language minority students: A theoretical framework* (pp. 3–49). Los Angeles, CA: Evaluation, Dissemination and Assessment Center, California State University.

Cummins, J. (1984). *Bilingualism and special education: Issues in assessment and pedagogy*. Clevedon, UK: Multilingual Matters.

Dalrymple, K.S. (1989). Well, what about his skills? Evaluation of whole language in middle school. In K.S. Goodman, Y.M. Goodman, & W.J. Hood (Eds.), *The whole language evaluation book* (pp. 111–130). Portsmouth, NH: Heinemann.

Downing, J. (1984). A source of cognitive confusion for beginning readers: Learning in a second language. *The Reading Teacher, 37*, 366–370.

Durán, R.P. (1983). *Hispanics' education and background: Predictors of college achievement*. New York: College Board.

Eaton, A.J. (1980). A psycholinguistic analysis of the oral reading miscues of selected field-dependent and field-independent native Spanish-speaking Mexican-American first-grade children. In *Outstanding dissertations in bilingual education* (pp. 15–28). Rosslyn, VA: National Clearinghouse for Bilingual Resources.

Edelsky, C., & Harman, S. (1988). One more critique of reading tests—with two differences. *English Education, 20*, 157–171.

Edwards, P.A., & García, G.E. (1991). Parental involvement in mainstream schools: An issue of equity. In M. Foster (Ed.), *Readings on equal education, Volume 11: Qualitative investigations into schools and schooling* (pp. 167–187). New York: AMS.

Foertsch, M., & Pearson, P.D. (1987, December). *Reading assessment in basal reading series and standardized tests*. Paper presented at the annual meeting of the National Reading Conference, St. Petersburg, FL.

García, G.E. (1988). *Factors influencing the English reading test performance of Spanish-English bilingual children*. Unpublished doctoral dissertation, University of Illinois, Urbana-Champaign.

García, G.E. (1991). Factors influencing the English reading test performance of Spanish-speaking Hispanic students. *Reading Research Quarterly, 26*, 371–392.

García, G.E., & Pearson, P.D. (1991a). Modifying reading instruction to maximize its effectiveness for all students. In M.S. Knapp & P.M. Shields (Eds.), *Better schooling for the children of poverty: Alternatives to conventional wisdom* (pp. 31–59). Berkeley, CA: McCutchan.

García, G.E., & Pearson, P.D. (1991b). The role of assessment in a diverse society. In E. Hiebert (Ed.), *Literacy for a diverse society: Perspectives, practices, and policies* (pp. 253–278). New York: Teachers College, Columbia University.

García, G.E., Pearson, P.D., & Jimenez, R.T. (1990). *The at-risk dilemma: A synthesis of reading research* (Study 2.2.3.3b). Urbana, IL: University of Illinois, Reading Research and Education Center.

Geneshi, C. (1985). Observing communicative performance in young children. In A. Jagger, & M.T. Smith-Burke, (Eds.), *Observing the language learner* (pp. 131–142). Newark, DE: International Reading Association.

Goodman, Y.M., Watson, D.J., & Burke, C.L. (1987). *Reading miscue inventory: Alternative procedures.* New York: Richard C. Owen.

Hall, W.S., Nagy, W.E., & Linn, R. (1984). *Spoken words: Effects of situation and social group on oral word usage and frequency.* Hillsdale, NJ: Erlbaum.

Hood, W.J. (1989). If the teacher comes over, pretend it's a telescope. In K.S. Goodman, Y.M. Goodman, & W.J. Hood (Eds.), *The whole language evaluation book* (pp. 27–42). Portsmouth, NH: Heinemann.

Hudelson, S. (Ed.). (1981). *Learning to read in different languages* (Papers in applied linguistics: Linguistics and literacy series, 1). Washington, DC: Center for Applied Linguistics.

Johnston, P. (1984). Prior knowledge and reading comprehension tests bias. *Reading Research Quarterly, 19,* 219–239.

Lee, J.F. (1986). On the use of the recall task to measure L2 reading comprehension. *Studies in Second Language Acquisition, 8,* 201–211.

Mägiste, E. (1979). The competing language systems of the multilingual: A developmental study of decoding and encoding processes. *Journal of Verbal Learning and Verbal Behavior, 18,* 79–89.

Modiano, N. (1973). *Indian education in the Chiapas Highlands.* New York: Holt, Rinehart.

Morrow, L.M. (1989). Using story retelling to develop comprehension. In D.K. Muth (Ed.), *Children's comprehension of text: Research into practice* (pp. 37–58). Newark, DE: International Reading Association.

Muth, D.K. (Ed.). (1989). *Children's comprehension of text: Research into practice.* Newark, DE: International Reading Association.

Rothman, R. (1991, June 12). Researchers say emphasis on testing too narrow, could set back reforms. *Education Week,* 25.

Routman, R. (1988). *Transitions: From literature to literacy.* Portsmouth, NH: Heinemann.

Royer, J.M., & Cunningham, D.J. (1981). On the theory and measurement of reading comprehension. *Contemporary Educational Psychology, 6,* 187–216.

Savignon, S.J. (1983). *Communicative competence—Theory and classroom practice: Texts and contexts in second language learning.* Reading, MA: Addison-Wesley.

Stallman, A.C., & Pearson, P.D. (1990). Formal measures of early literacy. In L.M. Morrow & J.K. Smith (Eds.), *Assessment for instruction in early literacy* (pp. 7–44). Englewood Cliffs, NJ: Prentice Hall.

Tierney, R.J., Readence, J.E., Dishner, E.K. (1990). *Reading strategies and practices: A Compendium* (3rd ed.). Boston, MA: Allyn & Bacon.

Troike, R.C. (1982). Zeno's paradox and language assessment. In S.S. Seidner (Ed.), *Issues of language assessment: Foundations and research* (Proceedings of the First Annual Language Assessment Institute, pp. 3–5). Springfield, IL: Illinois State Board of Education.

Valencia, S.W., McGinley, W., & Pearson, P. D. (1990). Assessing reading and writing: Building a more complete picture. In G.G. Duffy (Ed.), *Reading in the middle school* (2nd ed., pp. 124–146). Newark, DE: International Reading Association.

Valencia, S.W., & Pearson, P.D. (1987). Reading assessment: Time for a change. *The Reading Teacher, 40,* 726–732.

Wixson, K.K., Peters, C.W., Weber, E.M., & Roeber, E.D. (1987). New directions in statewide reading assessment. *The Reading Teacher, 40,* 726–732.

Eleanor Wall Thonis

Conclusion

The ESL Student: Reflections on the Present, Concerns for the Future

Schools in the United States began to address the needs of the growing numbers of students from diverse language backgrounds and cultures relatively recently. As educators prepare for a new century, research is helping them to better understand these students and to create classrooms that offer more effective instruction. New school environments make many demands on students who are not native speakers of English. These students usually do not have knowledge and skills in English, nor do they have an understanding of the school culture of their new country. They represent many diverse ethnic groups and bring to school the richness of many languages. Despite these strengths, they meet many difficulties as they are expected to cope with the acquisition of English in both oral and written form in an instructional program that has been designed for native English speakers. The assumption that they can use the materials and textbooks prepared for their English-speaking peers without modification frequently contributes to failure and anomie for these students.

Research shows that the social contexts in which language is acquired and used in the classroom are significant variables in gaining second-language proficiency. Differences in classrooms are critical for the promotion or inhibition of language development. Long (1990) believes that any theory that does not include the environmental features in which a second language is acquired must be considered incomplete or inadequate. He notes further that affective factors must also be included in the development of a comprehensive theory. He suggests that second-language acquisition is a multidimensional phenomenon that includes learner and environmental variables. Second-language learners present the range of differences that may be expected among students in any classroom. To these personal, linguistic, social, and cultural diversities must be added variations in previous schooling, native-language literacy, opportunities for instruction in English, rate of school transfer, and other significant experiences, both in and out of school.

Flood et al. (1991) pose the question: "In what ways should our new national insights into the need for multiethnic, multicultural education affect the teaching of reading?" Their concern is one of critical importance for language-minority students in many areas of the country. Instruction of these students in classes that emphasize drill and practice does not show much promise. These traditional approaches need to be abandoned for more innovative approaches. Instructional methods that reflect current theory have shifted from an emphasis on separate, isolated skills to an integration of listening, speaking, reading, writing, and thinking. This shift challenges curriculum writers and teachers to reorganize instruction with new and authentic approaches to language and literacy in mind. Such programs as Reading Recovery (Clay, 1985), the use of educational technology, and writing to read instead of the usual reading to write seem to hold promise. Other possible options are the following:

- *Conferences* with the teacher and one or more students have been found to be especially effective for improving students' writing.

- *Peer tutoring* gives students the opportunity to learn from other students who have already developed the strategies or skills.
- *Modeling* by the teacher or a capable peer shows students how reading and writing strategies can be used successfully.
- *Collaborative or cooperative learning* allows students to work and learn together.

Social interaction and peer cooperation make important contributions to proficiency in writing. Even though writers write in isolation most of the time, Glatthorn (1989) states that writing is a social and collaborative act. In addition, he notes that "when individuals interact with a stimulating environment in which the students have real problems to solve, there is a genuine quality to the writing purpose." This kind of classroom offers the students opportunities for more active participation in roles that allow them to "meditate, fantasize, talk, ask questions, observe, act parts, and create novel solutions." Another important feature of such classrooms is the attitude toward errors they promote. In these environments, errors are regarded as natural; they occur because the learner is trying out various strategies, and they are in fact useful for learners' development of skills.

Johnson (1991) also points out that second-language teaching and learning are embedded in a social context, and that individuals respond to this context in different ways. Except for moments of private reflection, meditation, or musing, language is used by people in social settings. This view of the function and purpose of language emphasizes the communicative competence of learners. Contemporary researchers are examining language as social behavior in a variety of social contexts.

The trend toward planned activities in pairs or small groups is an important one, if only for the opportunity it gives students to talk to one another. Classroom activities aim for communicative competence, and small-group work is conducive to achieving this. Note, though, that grouping alone does not provide all the answers to the complexities of communicative competence. Language is human behavior and occurs among people for particular reasons. In the microcosm of the school, language, both oral and written, promotes knowledge, skills, and values reflective of the larger society.

Savignon (1991) asks how form and function should be integrated to promote communicative competence. Appropriateness of language, an understanding of its pragmatic use, and sensitivity to the cultural characteristics of different speech communities present additional challenges to educators. These concerns and others like them reflect changes in the role of teachers and of students in working together toward the goal of communicative competence.

Language development and use do not happen in isolation, but are interdependent, interrelated, and mutually supportive. Students who are not native English speakers demonstrate a variety of skill levels in both oral and written English, and to accommodate student diversities, teachers must be imaginative and flexible. The following practical suggestions may be useful:

- To ensure comprehension, use an expressive voice, gestures, pantomime, objects, and pictures whenever possible in presenting lessons.

- To nurture self-esteem, display students' work in the classroom—drawings, writings, murals, messages, and other efforts.

- To achieve real communication, encourage conversations, role-playing, questioning, and other opportunities to send and receive actual messages.

- To allow for individual differences in readiness to produce speech, recognize that not all students will respond orally at the same time. Allow them as much listening time as they need.

- Remember that teachers must feel comfortable about the way they teach and may add, change, or omit parts of lessons as they interact with the students and materials. The approach should not be so prescriptive as to limit creativity.

- Keep in mind that, although at times activities are listed separately for convenience, listening, comprehension, speaking, reading, writing, and thinking are not isolated, separate mental activities. Classroom lessons involve multiple language skills, but not all students need to demonstrate them publicly at the same time and in the same manner.

In their work on creativity, Goleman et al. (1992) write about the "something within us that must be brought to life in something outside of us." The internal and the external work together to influence the attitudes and behaviors of students. The authors describe a school near Milan whose guiding principle is *"Niente senza gioia"*—nothing without joy. The staff foster an atmosphere where joy envelops students and teachers so that creativity and inventiveness may happen. Conversely, they deplore an environment that inhibits creativity, including creativity killers such as these:

- Surveillance—hovering over children.
- Evaluation—judging what children are doing.
- Rewards—using prizes excessively.
- Competition—putting children in a win-lose situation.
- Over-control—telling children exactly how to do things.
- Restricting Choice—assigning tasks regardless of children's interests.
- Pressure—establishing grandiose expectations.

Conclusion   **211**

To keep written language in perspective, the teacher should be cautious about written assignments. Progress in the acquisition of English is not totally dependent on reading and writing, especially at first. Older students who are developmentally mature may have greater success than younger ones in reading and writing activities.

Bruder and Henderson (1986) remind teachers that beginners in a new language do not have the metalanguage to talk about the tenses of verbs, the relationships in a grammatical structure, and other features of language. Students are often given tasks that require descriptions and analyses of language before they have acquired and used the language or have any real understanding of its terminology. Although grammar should not be a primary focus for beginners, its introduction and exploration may be relevant for more advanced students. Unfortunately, second-language lessons do not always make this distinction. Failure to respect the differences in their acquisition, use, and analysis of English may place impossible demands on students hindered by limited vocabulary, lack of practice, and poor knowledge of grammar.

Hernandez-Chavez (1984) and Dolson (1985) describe the depressing contrasts between majority- and minority-schooling environments in the United States. They note that (1) minority students come principally from a lower socioeconomic group; (2) their parents often have little control over the family's economic resources and are frequently unable to access social welfare resources; (3) home languages are not valued in schools; and (4) children may be alienated in both cultural settings. Clearly, these factors do not make a positive contribution to the schooling of minority students, nor do they promote the comfort levels necessary for second-language development.

Hiebert (1991) suggests that the social nature of reading and writing and the roles of both teachers and students are changing. Research continues to present ideas of how listening, speaking, reading, and writing may be deeply integrated in a mutually supportive manner in which fluency and literacy may flourish. Bermudez and Prater (1989) make a strong case for direct instruction to improve comprehension and retention. They believe that teachers should not assume that ESL students will have the ability to solve and organize their ideas purely on the basis of opportunities to brainstorm, cluster, or summarize. They suggest that ESL students especially need to think, read, and write in "an integrated manner as they are acquiring communicative skills in English." They also believe that writing opportunities will enhance the students' abilities in higher order thinking skills.

Contemporary research advocates flexibility in the sequence of skill instruction, focus on the active participation of learners, emphasis on a cooperative atmosphere, opportunity for self-direction, and nurturing of self-esteem. These will benefit all students but are essential for those who are working toward becoming fluent and literate in English as a second language. Further, a review of the language and literacy needs of language-minority students in schools designed for English speakers shows the importance of (1) the environment in which learning takes place; (2) the active role of the learners; (3) the integration of language skills; (4) the social context of learning; (5) an emphasis on thinking; and (6) authenticity of communication. The personal and social complexities of the situation for ESL students are leading educators to search further for answers to these pressing questions:

1. How do specific features of the classroom contribute to or detract from personal growth?
2. How can teachers best provide instruction for a diverse student body?
3. How can teachers promote a real integration of language skills?
4. How can the direct instruction necessary for ESL students be delivered in ways other than whole-class approaches?

Conclusion   **213**

5. How can teachers avoid contrived, artificial purposes for communication and instead offer real, authentic opportunities for students to use language?

6. How can teacher-education programs at all levels respond to the complex issues of training present and future teachers who staff classrooms where ESL students are enrolled?

7. What criteria are most important in selecting materials appropriate to the language and literacy skills of ESL students?

8. What measures are sufficiently comprehensive to evaluate student progress and program strengths?

9. How can measures to meet the instructional needs of ESL students be integrated into the curriculum?

10. To what extent is it possible to develop a school that truly reflects a multicultural, multilingual society?

These and many other unresolved issues continue to be major stumbling blocks on the road to improvement of language and literacy instruction for language-minority students. One constant remains in this era of change: the students are in the classrooms now in numbers that will continue to grow. Schools have a great responsibility to provide the best possible educational opportunities. *All* students are a significant part of every nation's future; they all deserve the collective energies and talents of all resources the schools can offer.

Opportunities to create language-rich classrooms are bounded only by the creativity of the teacher and students who share those classrooms. The value of such classrooms is evident in the way they communicate the importance of speech and print and the power of both. Learning to listen with comprehension, to speak with fluency, to read with understanding, and to write with style are abilities that nourish the growth of human beings. These skills provide students with precision instruments that enhance their reasoning abilities and intelligence. For students who are adding English to their native-language abilities, a literate environment offers a path to greater literacy.

Our present concerns must take into account that we are educating a citizenry that will inherit, not a restricted space on the globe, but a place in a global village. This world needs all the languages and all the literacies of all people. Literate environments are capable of carrying this message to all students of all languages.

References

Bermudez, A., & Prater, D. (1989). Evaluating the effectiveness of writing on the comprehension and retention of content reading. *NABE Annual Conference Journal, 1988–1989*, 151–156.

Bruder, M., & Henderson, R. (1986). *Beginning reading in English as a second language.* Washington, DC: Center for Applied Linguistics.

Clay, M. (1985). *The early detection of reading difficulties.* Portsmouth, NH: Heinemann.

Dolson, D. (1985). Bilingualism and scholastic performance: The literature revisited. *NABE Journal, 10*(1), 1–35.

Flood, J., Jensen, J.M., Lapp, D., & Squire, J.R. (Eds.). (1991). Six major issues in the language arts. In *Handbook of research on teaching the English language arts.* New York: Macmillan.

Glatthorn, A. (1989). Thinking, writing, and reading: Making connections. In D. Lapp, J. Flood, & N. Farnan (Eds.), *Content area reading and learning* (pp. 283–296). Englewood Cliffs, NJ: Prentice Hall.

Goleman, D., Kaufman, P., & Ray, M. (1992). *The creative spirit.* New York: Penguin.

Hernandez-Chavez, E. (1984). The inadequacy of English immersion education as an educational approach for language minority students in the United States. In *Studies on immersion.* Sacramento, CA: California Department of Education.

Hiebert, E. (1991). Literacy contexts and literacy processes. *Language Arts, 68*, 134–139.

Johnson, D. (1991). Some observations on progress in research in second language learning and teaching. In M. McGroaty & C. Faltis (Eds.), *Language in school and society: Politics and pedagogy.* Berlin: de Gruyter.

Author Index

Note: An "f" following an index entry indicates that the citation may be found in a figure, a "t" that it may be found in a table.

McGinley, W., 188, 205
McLaren, P., 72, 81
McLaughlin, B., 88, 105
McNeil, J.D., 172, 178
Meredith, R., 68, 80
Met, M., 91, 106
Meyer, B.J.F., 175, 178
Modiano, N., 185, 204
Mohan, B.A., 52, 56, 61, 91, 102, 105
Morrow, L.M., 194, 204
Muth, D.K., 194, 204

N
Nagy, W.E., 117, 127, 184, 204
Nakajima, K., 60
National Alliance of Business, 12, 20
National Assessment of Educational Progress, 10, 20
National Center for Education Statistics, 9, 10, 20
National Center for Health Statistics, 13, 20
National Clearinghouse for Bilingual Education, 91, 105
National Coalition of Advocates for Students, 12, 20
Nattinger, J.R., 86, 105
Northcutt, L., 91, 105

O
Office of Bilingual Education and Minority Language Affairs, 1, 5
Ogbu, J.U., 53, 61, 159, 179
Ogle, D.S., 105, 167, 169f, 179
O'Hare, W.P., 13, 21
Olsen, L., 1, 2, 5, 18, 21
Olson, D.R., 39, 61
O'Malley, J.M., 1, 5, 84, 86, 90, 91, 92, 95, 102, 104, 105, 106, 117, 126
Ortiz, A.A., 39, 61

Oshiro, M.E., 150, 155
Ovando, C.J., 85, 88, 106, 159, 179

P
Palincsar, A.S., 90, 92, 94, 103, 105, 106
Paris, S.G., 90, 106
Paulston, C.B., 71, 81
Pearson, P.D., 138, 154, 181, 182, 183, 184, 185, 187, 188, 189, 190, 193, 199, 201, 203, 204, 205
Peregoy, S.F., 137, 144, 146, 154, 156
Peters, C.W., 205
Peterson, B., 119, 127
Piper, T., 139, 156
Prater, D., 212, 214
Pressley, M., 92, 106
Pritchard, R., 138, 156

R
Ramey, D.R., 51, 58, 61
Ramirez, J.D., 51, 58, 61
Ramírez, M., 31, 35
Ray, M., 214
Read, C., 111, 127
Readence, J.E., 194, 197, 205
Reed, L., 157
Richards, J.C., 85, 86, 87, 106
Rigg, P., 89, 99, 106, 112, 127, 137, 156
Rodgers, T.S., 85, 86, 87, 106
Roeber, E.D., 205
Rosenblatt, L.M., 138, 152, 156
Rothman, R., 180, 204
Routman, R., 195, 196, 199, 200, 204
Royer, J.M., 180, 205
Rueda, R., 45, 61

S
Salisbury, R., 148, 156
Savignon, S.J., 86, 87, 106, 183,

Subject Index

that support curriculum, 123-124, 129-130; whose illustrations support meaning, 120-121, 129

C

GRAMMAR TRANSLATION METHOD: 85

GROUP CHARTS: 191-192

GROUP RESOURCE ACCULTURATION: 25, 30-33

H

HOW QUESTIONS: use of, 177

I

IMMIGRANT EDUCATION PROGRAM: 19

IMMIGRATION: and public school enrollment, 12-13

INDIVIDUAL CHARTS: 191-192

INFORMATION: relating, 175-177

INSTRUCTION: sheltered, 91. *See also* Reading instruction; Teaching English as a second language

INSTRUCTIONAL APPROACHES: 82-107; CALLA, 91-94; communicative, 86-87; for different students, 100-103; ESL, 84-94; future directions, 177-178; language experience, 89; natural, 86, 87; for reading, 87-90; whole language, 89-90

INSTRUCTIONAL PROGRAMS: developing, 159-162. *See also* ESL programs

INTERACTION: communicative, 45-46; social contexts for, 74-77; with vocabulary in context, 172-173

INTERGROUP UNDERSTANDING ACCULTURATION: 25, 27-30

INTERLANGUAGE: 136

INTERPRETATION SYSTEMS: 136

J

JOURNALS: 167; dialogue, 151-153, 153f. *See also* Logs

K

KEY VISUALS: use of, 56-57. *See also* Visuals

KID-WATCHING: 78

KNOWLEDGE: linking to new concepts and ideas, 167-170; prereading activities related to, 164-170; tapping, focusing, and building on, 164-170; writing activities that focus, 166-167

K-W-L: *See* Linking prior knowledge to new concepts and ideas

L

LANGUAGE: contextualized and decontextualized, 39-40; patterned, using, 140-141; primary, role of, 160-161

LANGUAGE ACQUISITION: classroom principles for, 78; cognitive processes, 48, 50; linguistic processes, 48, 49-50; modeling and teaching strategies of, 97-98; social processes, 48-49. *See also* English acquisition; Literacy acquisition; Second-language acquisition

LANGUAGE DEVELOPMENT: ESL, 161-162; suggestions for, 209-210. *See also* Literacy development

LANGUAGE EXPERIENCE APPROACH: 89

LANGUAGE INTERACTION: social contexts for, 74-77

LANGUAGE LEARNERS: *See* Second-language learners

LANGUAGE LEARNING: *See* English acquisition; Language acquisition; Second-language acquisition

MULTILINGUAL CLASSROOMS: self-esteem and literacy in, 65-81; theme cycles in, 76f, 76-77. *See also* Classrooms

MULTIMEDIA PRESENTATIONS: pre-reading activities with, 165-166

MULTIPLE TEXTS: using, 143-144

N

NATIONAL TESTS: 180
NATURAL APPROACH: 86, 87

O

OBSERVATION: classroom, 191-193
ORAL-MISCUE ANALYSIS: 193
ORAL READING: tape-recordings of, 195-196
OUTLINING: 175-177; array, 176f, 177; radial, 176f, 177

P

PARENTS: involvement of, 100
PATTERNED LANGUAGE: using, 140-141
PEER TUTORING: 208
PHONICS INSTRUCTION: 88-89
PREJUDICES: linguistic, 38
PREREADING ACTIVITIES: related to background knowledge, 164-170
PRIMARY LANGUAGE: role of, 160-161
PRIOR KNOWLEDGE: linking to new concepts and ideas, 167-170; writing activities that focus, 166-167
PROGRAMS: basal reading, tests from, 187; bilingual, funding for, 19; Bilingual Education (Title VII), 19; Emergency Immigrant Education, 19; instructional, developing, 159-162; Tran-

sitional Program for Refugee Children, 19. *See also* ESL programs
PROMPTS: written, 167
PUBLIC SCHOOL ENROLLMENT: contributing factors, 12-13; of LEP students, 14-15, 17t-18t. *See also* Student enrollment

Q

QUESTIONS: use of, 177
QUICK-WRITES: 166-167

R

RADIALS: 176f, 177
READERS: basal, 115-116
READING: comprehending through, 135-158; daily, 97; for different purposes, 98; oral, tape-recordings of, 195-196; as preparation for writing, 139-144; teaching, 101-102; using, 141-143; and writing, 138-153; writing as preparation for, 144-145
READING-ACHIEVEMENT TESTS: standardized, 185-186. *See also* Tests
READING INSTRUCTION: approaches to, 87-90; CALLA strategies, 93; code-based or phonics, 88-89; materials for, 108-131; options, 207-208. *See also* Teaching English as a second language
READING LOGS: 196
READING MATERIALS: 108-131; criteria for selecting, 112-113; to support literacy acquisition, 113-118; using, 125-126
READING PRACTICES: that support comprehension, 139

READING PROGRAMS: basal, tests from, 187
READING READINESS TESTS: 184-185
READING-RESPONSE LOGS: 196-197
READING TESTS: standardized, 180-181; statewide, 187-188
REAL WORLD PRINT: 114-115
RECORDS: anecdotal, 191
REFUGEE CHILDREN: transitional program for, 19
REFUGEE EXPERIENCE: books about, 131
RELATING INFORMATION: 175-177
RESEARCH-BASED STRATEGIES: 135-158
RETELLING STORIES: 194-195

S

SCHOOLS: impact of increased enrollment on, 16-18. See also Student enrollment
SECOND-LANGUAGE ACQUISITION: cognitive processes, 48, 50; of English, 36-62; individual differences in, 45-52, 52-58; input and attributes in, 46, 47f; linguistic processes, 48, 49-50; social processes, 48-49; time required for, 42-45, 43f. See also Language acquisition
SECOND-LANGUAGE LEARNERS: cultural constraint of success for, 71-72; meeting language and literacy needs of, 159-177. See also ESL students; LEP students; Minority students
SELF-ESTEEM: 65-81; beliefs relevant to, 68-70; classroom principles for, 78; curriculum for, 72-78; language environment for, 73-74; and literacy development, 67-70; literacy environment for, 73-74; suggestions for building, 209
SELF-EVALUATION: student, 100
SEMANTIC FEATURE ANALYSIS: 171, 172f
SEMANTIC MAPPING: 145-148, 171-172, 173f
SEQUENCING: in expository text, 175
SHAPES: semantic feature analysis of, 171, 172f
SHELTERED INSTRUCTION: 91
SITUATIONAL CULTURAL APPROPRIATENESS: 27
SKILL INSTRUCTION: flexibility in, 212
SKILLS: first-language, 95-96
SOCIAL CONTEXTS: for language interaction, 74-77
SOCIAL PROCESSES: 48-49
SPEECH: suggestions for, 209
STANDARDIZED READING-ACHIEVEMENT TESTS: 185-186
STANDARDIZED READING TESTS: 180-181
STATE FUNDING: 19
STATEWIDE READING TESTS: 187-188
STORY GRAMMAR SHEET: using, 142, 142f
STORY RETELLING: 194-195
STORY TELLING OR WRITING: 195
STUDENT ENROLLMENT: changes in, 9-21; contributing factors, 12-13; increased, impact on schools, 16-18; language issues, 13-16; of LEP students, 14-15, 17t-18t; by race/ethnicity, 9-10, 11t
STUDENTS: See ESL students; LEP students; Minority students
STUDENT-TEACHER CONFERENCES: 200-201, 207
SUCCESS: as cultural constraint, 71-72

SUMMARIZING: 148-150

T

TALK: books that invite, 121-122

TAPE-RECORDINGS: of oral reading, 195-196

TEACHER OBSERVATION: 191

TEACHING ENGLISH AS A SECOND LANGUAGE: COMMUNICATIVE (CLT), 86-87; content-based approaches, 90-94; future directions, 177-178; implications of individual differences in English acquisition for, 52-58; instructional approaches, 84-94, 100-103; literacy issues, 135-137; materials for, 108-131; options, 207-208; principles, 53-58; procedures, 82-107; research-based strategies, 135-158; strategies, 97-98, 158-179; suggestions for, 95-100, 210; use of key visuals in, 56-57

TELLING STORIES: 195

TESTS: from basal reading programs, 187; formal, 182-188; language-proficiency, 183-184; national, 180; reading readiness, 184-185; standardized, 185-186; statewide, 187-188

TEST SCORES: 180-181

TEXTBOOKS: 115-117; content area, 116-117

TEXT(S): analyzing, 162-164; multiple, using, 143-144; outlining, 175-177, 176f. *See also* Expository text(s)

THEME CYCLES: 76f, 76-77

THINK-ALOUDS: 197-199

TITLE VII: *See* Bilingual Education

TRANSITIONAL PROGRAM FOR REFUGEE CHILDREN: 19

TUTORING: peer, 208

U

UNDERACHIEVEMENT: 10-12

V

VISUALS: prereading activities with, 164-165; use of, 56-57

VOCABULARY: in context, interacting with, 172-173

VOCABULARY DEVELOPMENT: 170-173; example activities for, 171-173

W

WEBBING: 145-148, 147f, 148f

WHOLE LANGUAGE APPROACHES: 89-90

WH QUESTIONS: use of, 177

WRITING: books that give framework for, 122-123, 129; by children, 113-114; comprehending through, 135-158; journal, 167; as preparation for reading, 144-145; reading and, 138-153; reading as preparation for, 139-144; stories, 195; teaching, 99-100; using, 141-143; using multiple texts for, 143-144; using predictable books and patterned language for, 140-141; using reading, writing, and discussion for, 141-143

WRITING ACTIVITIES: that focus prior knowledge, 166-167

WRITING FOLDERS: 199-200

WRITING PRACTICES: that support comprehension, 139

WRITTEN COMMUNICATION: 150-151

WRITTEN PROMPTS: 167